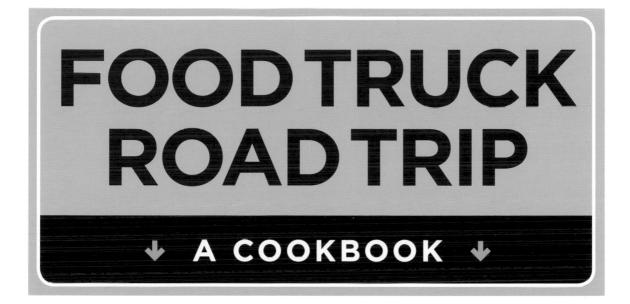

FOOD TRUCK ROAD TRIP

A COOKBOOK

MORE THAN 100 RECIPES COLLECTED FROM
THE BEST STREET FOOD VENDORS COAST TO COAST

KIM PHAM & PHILIP SHEN

creators of BehindtheFoodCarts.com, named the Best Culinary Travel Blog by *Saveur* magazine

WITH TERRI PHILLIPS

PAGE STREET
PUBLISHING CO.

PAGE STREET
PUBLISHING CO.

Copyright © 2014 Kim Pham, Philip Shen with Terri Phillips

First published in 2014 by
Page Street Publishing Co.
27 Congress Street, Suite 103
Salem, MA 01970
www.pagestreetpublishing.com

Distributed by Macmillan; sales in Canada by The Canadian Manda Group; distribution in Canada by The Jaguar Book Group.

17   16   15   14   1   2   3   4   5

ISBN-13: 978-1-62414-080-8
ISBN-10: 1-62414-080-7

Library of Congress Control Number: 2014902460

Cover and book design by Page Street Publishing Co.
Photography by KIM+PHIL Photography

Printed and bound in China

Page Street is proud to be a member of 1% for the Planet. Members donate one percent of their sales to one or more of the over 1,500 environmental and sustainability charities across the globe who participate in this program.

DEDICATIONS

KIM: To my parents, Nancy and Duc, and my brother, Long, for always supporting me.

PHIL: To my mom, Annie, whom I miss every day, for being a foodie before
the term foodie existed.

TERRI: To my husband, Justin, for always believing in whatever I think of next.

CONTENTS

FOREWORD

The story of modern food trucks in America is a big one, a sweeping epic involving everything from the 2008 financial crisis to the simultaneous rise of social media and Internet food culture. But inside every truck and behind every cart there's a person—sometimes two or three—who has a story that's far more intimate. Ask anyone why they're working on a food truck and I guarantee you'll get an awfully good tale about the road that led them there. These stories tell us where our food is coming from, who the people are who are serving it to us, and also what exactly it is that we're really doing when we sweat under a New Orleans summer sun waiting for a paper tray of oh-so-worth-it boudin-filled pot stickers.

That's why what Kim Pham and Phil Shen are doing with *Behind the Food Carts* is so fantastic, and so essential. I first became fans of theirs online, as an avid reader of their blog behindthefoodcarts .com, and I was honored to be part of the committee that named them the Best Culinary Travel Blog in *Saveur* magazine's 2013 Best Food Blog Awards. As I've gotten to know Kim and Phil in real life as well, it's become increasingly obvious that they—along with their writing partner Terri Phillips—are more than hobbyist bloggers; they're true storytellers. They go in deep with the men and women on the other end of the truck-side counter, finding out where they come from, what they love, and what's on the menu, and then sharing it all with us through beautiful words and images.

I can't remember the first time I bought food from a truck, but I do remember the first time I stood in front of one and realized that in doing so I was participating in one of the great food movements of the era. I'd just come face to face with New York's Treats Truck, a silver van bearing a retro logo, from which chef Kim Ima peddles cookies, brownies, and other sweets to delighted masses who queue a dozen deep. It was a novelty then, but in the years since, America has become speckled with food trucks, slinging everything from French toast to Thai green curry, and this book is a thrilling—and appetite-whetting—survey of food that's being cooked in galley-narrow, rickety-wheeled kitchens throughout the country. Imbued as it is with Kim, Phil and Terri's spirit of discovery and celebration, it's a beautiful document of real American food culture—not the rarefied restaurant cooking that might, over time, trickle its way down to the rest of us, but the food that we're eating, all of us, right now, while loving every bite of it.

—Helen Rosner

Helen Rosner is the Executive Digital Editor for *Saveur* magazine

INTRODUCTION

BY PHIL SHEN

Wow, how did we get here? Kim and I packed up our bags and threw everything into my tiny VW Golf in the summer of 2009. We moved from our native sunny SoCal to perpetually overcast Portland, Oregon. It was a decision done on a whim, fulfilling a craving for adventure and a fresh start in a new city. The dream was to become self-sufficient full-time photographers. But of course, our savings ran low in a matter of months and we struggled to make it as just photographers. I took a full-time job at a call center to help pay the bills and keep the dream of pursuing our passion for photography alive.

Growing up, I spent many summers abroad vacationing in Asia. I really loved the energy of the night market scene in Taiwan. Hungry customers sought out street food vendors selling hot, delicious treats. I often wondered why such a culture didn't exist in America. Little did I know that I happened to be in the perfect city for experiencing the food culture I sought. As the photo gigs sporadically came in, we became enamored with the Portland food cart scene. Our weekends were spent exploring the various food truck pods around town, which were filled with countless different carts serving everything from mac and cheese to foie gras.

As we ate from food cart to food cart, we couldn't help but notice the many proprietors who ran these tiny kitchens. It was often just one person taking the order, cooking the food and serving the dish. We became really curious about these passionate people who were putting their sweat and tears into their business. We were always on the lookout for photography projects that we could put our passion behind. It was from Kim's beautiful mind that the idea came to start a food blog. It was the best of both worlds for us—our love of food and capturing images.

No one decides to run a food cart for the glamour. Running a food cart means standing in a borderline claustrophobic space, sometimes with up to four other people, with a hot grill or oven for hours. It's sweating it out on hot days with temperatures soaring up to 120°F (49°C) and watching the clouds for rain. It means dealing with equipment failure, limited storage and competition for parking spots. It's figuring out how to challenge preconceived notions of the "roach coach" and serve high-end, restaurant-quality dishes out of a small box.

And yet more and more people are joining the food cart community every day. The chefs in this book come from backgrounds of every color. We've spoken to a former Ivy-League educated lawyer, a death metal sound technician, a plumber of twenty years and restaurant veterans with Michelin star experience under their belts. Some have paid their dues in prestigious culinary institutions and some have gone through their college years eating nothing but grilled cheese sandwiches. Some highlight the food for which their area is known, and some share dishes their parents and grandparents prepared in their home countries.

Food carts come in various forms. There are food carts circled in wagon train–type food pods, food stands in markets and mobile food trucks vying for a spot on the busy streets of their city. But, we've found one unifying characteristic in each person manning these tiny kitchens: passion. They're all driven by the desire to share the food they love. It's not a hobby or something that may be fun to try out; it's a necessity, like breathing and sleeping. They have a restless need to communicate their very selves to the rest of the world through their cooking, and they wouldn't want to be doing anything else.

The idea behind our blog was simple. Let's not focus on just creating a food porn blog; instead, let's focus on the people behind the scenes. From Ryan Carpenter making smoothies with a bicycle-powered blender in Portland, Oregon, to Mikala Brennan introducing citizens of Washington, D.C. to Hawaiian ahi poke. These are people who have great stories to tell. It was not until we met Terri, a writer, that we were able to complete the team. We instantly knew she needed to join our Behind the Food Carts blog to ensure that we do our best in narrating people's stories with words to accompany our photos.

This book is all about them. When we took on this project, we were determined to personally speak with every single chef or owner of sixty-three carts in twelve cities: Portland, Oregon; San Francisco and Los Angeles, California; Austin, Texas; New Orleans, Louisiana; Charlotte, Raleigh and Durham, North Carolina; Atlanta, Georgia; Philadelphia, Pennsylvania; Washington, D.C.; Minneapolis, Minnesota and New York City. Does a two-week, transcontinental road trip sound a little crazy? Maybe, but they deserve it. We wanted to hear their stories and get a feel for the passion that keeps them flipping over that "Open" sign every day.

Each chapter kicks off with an introduction by Phil and a full food truck story by Terri, and each recipe features a personal tidbit or anecdote from the contributor. These recipes are not "inspired by" or "based on" the menus of the food trucks featured; they're direct from the chefs themselves. You may not be able to travel to Love Balls Bus in Austin, Texas for Garlic Yaki Onigiri, but you can sear some up in your home kitchen and taste Chef Gabe Rothschild's drive and dedication for yourself.

We've told numerous food cart stories on our blog, and we're honored to be part of such an amazing community. We're elated to help promote a burgeoning industry filled with creativity. This blog has been a labor of love for us, and there have been countless times we've wanted to call it quits. But every time we go to another owner and hear his or her story, we're inspired to keep trucking along. You always hear that following your passion will yield the greatest rewards. We can't emphasize how true that's been for us. We're humbled by the opportunity to tell a little bit of our story, but we're more excited for you to hear the stories of these chefs and owners who have inspired us to make this book.

CHAPTER 1

AMERICAN COMFORT: CLASSICS WITH A TWIST

When we were first approached to do a book, we knew we wanted to do something on a national scale. Maybe we were overly ambitious, but because you're reading this now, maybe we pulled it off. The one common theme we saw as we looked across the country planning our book was that a lot of carts and trucks are focused on dishing out some form of American comfort food. Whether it is a spin on a burger or fried chicken, these are familiar foods that tug at people's hearts.

As we brainstormed, we found it hard to just narrow our focus to American comfort food. Comfort food means something different to so many people across America. A kid like me growing up in LA thinks of burritos, and a kid growing up for Louisiana finds comfort in gumbo. And as a second-generation Asian-American, I grew up shunning my culture for fear of not being seen as a "real" American. It's taken me a long time, but now I miss some of those Taiwanese dishes that I ate as a kid and have accepted them as part of my comfort food repertoire.

We can endlessly debate the definition of "American food," but this chapter pays homage to our initial concept. It's about those classic dishes that you think of, with a twist. Whether it's barbecued pulled pork in a taco from Hill Country Barbecue in Redwood City, California, or a French toast breakfast sandwich from the Egg Carton in Portland, Oregon, these are recipes that will remind you of some of your favorite comfort foods. It doesn't matter what we label it—we just want these dishes to put a smile on your face.

THE URBAN OVEN—SCOTT TREMONTI
LOS ANGELES, CALIFORNIA

Chef Scott Tremonti blames his single-minded pursuit of wood-fired pizza perfection on a pie from Pizzeria Bianco in Phoenix, Arizona. "I had good pizza before, but when you had Chris Bianco's pizza, it was almost like a religious experience," he says. "That was my first experience with a wood-fired oven." Having had an authentic, artisanal, Napoli-style pizza, Scott couldn't go back.

After moving to Seattle, Scott began to experiment with recipes to re-create the experience, going so far as to jimmy the lock on his home oven during the cleaning cycle to reach that elusive 800°F (427°C) temperature. He eventually purchased a wood-fired oven and spent a couple of years baking pizzas for a group of very lucky friends before starting his own food truck, The Urban Oven.

Now, The Urban Oven can be found roaming the streets of LA, bringing perfectly charred crusts, high-quality ingredients and an authentic experience to the masses. "It starts with the crust," Scott explains. "The crust is everything. That, to me, is the foundation. You talk to people that have had an experience with pizza, they always talk about the crust first. It's your canvas, it's where you start, it's 90 percent of your whole experience." Scott ferments his dough for no fewer than 24 hours, and he's careful not to overhandle it to create a light, airy, crispy dough perfect for showcasing the locally sourced, well-balanced toppings, such as the unexpected but delightful combination of prosciutto and grape.

PROSCIUTTO AND GRAPE PIZZA

THE URBAN OVEN—SCOTT TREMONTI—LOS ANGELES, CA

MAKES TWO 14" (35.6CM) PIZZAS

"For me, balance is really important," Scott Tremonti explains. "I do a lot of pizzas with the sweet and savories." This pizza, with buttery fontina cheese, sweet caramelized grapes and slightly bitter rosemary, perfectly captures Scott's ideal of balance.

BASIC DOUGH (MAKES 2)
2 tsp (6g) yeast (we use Fleischmann's yeast)
1 cup (236ml) lukewarm water
2 tsp (10g) salt
1 ¾ cups (174g) flour

1 cup (130g) fontina cheese
12 red grapes, halved
1 tsp rosemary
2 tbsp (30ml) olive oil
8 slices prosciutto crudo, thinly sliced

To make the dough, in a mixer fitted with a paddle attachment, combine the yeast and water and mix on low speed for 5 minutes. Meanwhile, combine the salt and flour in a separate bowl.

When the yeast has dissolved, add one-third of the flour and salt mixture and mix on low speed until incorporated. Stop the mixer and scrape the sides of the bowl. Add another one-third of the flour mixture to the bowl and once it has been incorporated, mix on high speed for 30 seconds. Stop the mixer and scrape the sides of the bowl. Add the remaining flour mixture and mix on medium speed until combined. The dough should be sticky, but not lumpy.

Transfer the dough to a floured, airtight container and allow it to rise for 24 hours. The dough will double in size, so be sure to use a large container.

After the dough has risen, transfer it to a lightly floured surface and divide in half. Roll each half into a ball, cover and allow it to rise at room temperature for 2 hours.

Preheat the oven broiler to high and place 2 baking stones in the oven for 1 hour. When the dough is ready, flatten each ball of dough one at a time on a lightly floured work surface into a 14-inch (35.6cm) round, taking care to preserve a 1-inch (2.5cm) lip around the edge. Place each dough circle on a baking stone.

Sprinkle half the fontina, grapes and rosemary on each pizza and drizzle half the olive oil on top. Place the pizzas in the oven and bake for 5 to 6 minutes. The edge of the crust should begin to puff up and you'll notice small dark brown spots begin to form on the bottom, also known as "leoparding." The cheese should also be melted. When the crust has achieved the desired browning and the pizza feels firm on the peel, it's ready to remove from the oven.

Remove the pizzas from the oven and top with half the prosciutto crudo, then slice and serve.

BACON AND SWEET ONION PIZZA

THE URBAN OVEN—SCOTT TREMONTI—LOS ANGELES, CA

MAKES TWO 14" (35.6CM) PIZZAS

"It's all about creating an experience around eating the food," says Scott. We think every bite of this pizza is an event in itself. Savory applewood-smoked bacon and sweet onion harmonize perfectly for a pizza that seems simple on the surface, but has a sophisticated depth of flavor.

BASIC DOUGH (MAKES 2)

2 tsp (6g) yeast (we use Fleischmann's yeast)

1 cup (236ml) lukewarm water

2 tsp (10g) salt

1 ¾ cups (174g) flour

½ cup (118ml) pomodoro sauce

⅔ cup (86g) mozzarella

6 strips applewood-smoked bacon, cooked

½ cup (32g) sliced sweet onion

To make the dough, in a mixer fitted with a paddle attachment, combine the yeast and water and mix on low speed for 5 minutes. Meanwhile, combine the salt and flour in a separate bowl.

When the yeast has dissolved, add one-third of the flour and salt mixture and mix on low speed until incorporated. Stop the mixer and scrape the sides of the bowl. Add another one-third of the flour mixture to bowl and once it has been incorporated, mix on high speed for 30 seconds. Stop the mixer and scrape the sides of the bowl. Add the remaining flour mixture and mix on medium speed until combined. The dough should be sticky, but not lumpy.

Transfer the dough to a floured, airtight container and allow it to rise for 24 hours. The dough will double in size, so be sure to use a large container.

After the dough has risen, transfer it to a lightly floured surface and divide in half. Roll each half into a ball, cover and allow it to rise at room temperature for 2 hours.

Preheat the oven broiler to high and place 2 baking stones in the oven for 1 hour. When the dough is ready to use, flatten each ball of dough one at a time on a lightly floured work surface into a 14-inch (35.6cm) round, taking care to preserve a 1-inch (2.5cm) lip around the edge. Place each dough circle on a baking stone.

Pour half the pomodoro sauce in the center of each pizza crust and, using the back of a ladle, spread in a circular motion until the crust is lightly covered, leaving 1 to 1 ½ inches (2.5 to 3.8cm) clear at the edge. Sprinkle with half the mozzarella, bacon and sweet onion on top.

Place the pizzas in the oven and bake for 5 to 6 minutes. The edge of the crust should begin to puff up and you'll notice small dark brown spots begin to form on the bottom, also known as "leoparding." The cheese should also be melted. When the crust has achieved the desired browning and the pizza feels firm on the peel, it's ready. Remove from the oven, slice and serve.

JALAPEÑO CORN CAKES

BIG D'S GRUB TRUCK—DENNIS KUM—NEW YORK, NY

MAKES 12 CORN CAKES

Dennis of Big D's Grub Truck in New York started his culinary career at the tender age of nine, mostly because he wasn't too fond of what his mom was cooking. But there is one particular dish that brings up happy childhood memories, jalapeño corn cakes. "This was a recipe I got from my friend's grandmother," he recalls. "She used to cook it for us when we were growing up, and I loved it." With a hint of sweetness, these corn cakes are good enough to be enjoyed alone or with eggs for what Dennis describes as a well-rounded breakfast. These cakes have a subtle sweetness to them, so no syrup required.

¾ cup (75g) flour

⅓ cup (33g) masa

⅓ cup (57g) cornmeal

¼ cup (48g) sugar

1 tbsp (12g) baking powder

Pinch of salt

1 cup (237ml) milk

2 eggs

¼ cup (59ml) oil

1 cup (151g) corn, frozen and thawed or canned and drained

⅔ cup (114g) canned, chopped jalapeños

In a large bowl, combine the flour, masa, cornmeal, sugar, baking powder and salt. Blend the milk, eggs and oil in a separate small bowl. Pour the wet ingredients into the dry and mix with a large spoon until incorporated. Do not overmix (lumps are okay). Fold in the corn and jalapeños.

Heat a large, lightly oiled griddle over medium heat. After the griddle is hot, pour ⅓ cup (80g) of the mixture on at a time. Brown for 1 or 2 minutes on each side. If the cakes are browning too fast, turn down the heat a little.

Place the corn cakes on a towel-lined plate and cover with an additional towel to keep warm.

FOPO CRISTO

THE EGG CARTON—SARAH ARKWRIGHT—PORTLAND, OR

MAKES 2 SANDWICHES

Portland is a city of brunchers. In that bewitching hour between breakfast and lunch, every restaurant serving brunch features long lines of hungry citizens. The Egg Carton prides itself on making a damn good brunch. Sarah and Tim Arkwright—a server-turned-lawyer and a former teacher with a retail background—recommends the FoPo Cristo: French toast with fried egg, Cheddar cheese, Canadian bacon, sweet and spicy mustard and strawberry jam.

FRENCH TOAST BATTER

3 large eggs

½ cup (118ml) half-and-half

1 tsp vanilla extract

1 tsp pumpkin pie spice

Pinch of salt

1 tbsp (14g) unsalted butter

4 slices Texas toast bread

1 tsp sweet and spicy mustard (we use Beaver)

2 tbsp (31g) strawberry jam

2 slices medium Cheddar cheese (we use Tillamook)

4 slices bacon, cooked

6 slices Canadian bacon, cooked

2 eggs, cooked over-easy

Powdered sugar, for serving

To make the French toast batter, lightly whisk the eggs in a large bowl until the yolks are incorporated. Add the half-and-half, vanilla, pumpkin pie spice and a pinch of salt and whisk until blended. Pour the batter into a container with a flat bottom large enough to soak the Texas toast.

Heat a large griddle over medium-high heat. Place the butter on the griddle. Let it melt and cover the surface.

Dunk each slice of Texas toast into the French toast batter. Let each slice sit in the batter for about 10 seconds to soak up the liquid, then place each slice on the hot griddle.

Let the toast cook for 1 to 2 minutes, or until browned. The texture of the browned side should be slightly firm, not soggy. Flip the bread and brown the same way on the other side and set aside.

To assemble the sandwich, put ½ teaspoon of the mustard on 2 slices of the French toast. Then add 1 tablespoon (15g) of the jam on top of the mustard. Complete each sandwich with 1 slice of cheese, 2 slices of bacon, 3 slices of Canadian bacon and 1 over-easy egg, and top with the remaining French toast. Sprinkle with the powdered sugar. Things could get messy, so serve with a knife and fork.

THE GOOD MORNING

FRENCHEEZE FOOD TRUCK—JASON ROBINSON KING—NEW ORLEANS, LA

MAKES 2 SANDWICHES

Although Jason King's New Orleans–based truck Frencheeze specializes in grilled cheese, it's got a firm handle on another quintessential comfort food: French toast. With mascarpone, Nutella and syrup-infused strawberries, this French toast starts your day with a dash of true decadence. It'll be a good morning indeed.

1 pint (300g) strawberries

1 ½ cups (355ml) maple syrup

4 eggs

⅔ cup (158ml) milk

2 tsp (5g) cinnamon

2 tsp (4g) freshly grated orange zest (optional)

¼ cup (59ml) Triple Sec (optional)

4 thick slices 2-day-old bread, better if slightly stale

8 tbsp (115g) butter

8 tbsp (115g) Nutella

½ cup (115g) mascarpone cheese

1 tbsp (15g) raw sugar, for garnish

To make the syrup-infused strawberries, soak the strawberries in the maple syrup, in a bowl, at room temperature for 30 to 45 minutes or in the refrigerator overnight.

In a bowl, beat the eggs, milk and cinnamon together. Add the orange zest and Triple Sec. Whisk until well blended. Pour into a shallow bowl. Dip each slice of bread into the egg mixture, allowing the bread to soak up some of the mixture.

Melt 1 tablespoon (15g) of butter per slice of bread in a large skillet over medium-high heat. Add as many slices of bread on the skillet as will fit. Fry for 3 to 4 minutes, until brown on both sides, flipping the bread when necessary.

Spread half the Nutella on the bottom piece of French toast. Spread half the mascarpone on the top piece of toast. Place half the strawberries along with some of the syrup on the bottom piece of toast and add the top slice, mascarpone side facing in. Sprinkle raw sugar on the top piece of toast and crystallize with a hand torch. Repeat for the second sandwich.

BISCUITS WITH COUNTRY SAUSAGE GRAVY

PIE PUSHERS—MIKE HACKER—DURHAM, NC

SERVES 8 TO 10

We honestly can't think of anything more comforting than fluffy, freshly baked biscuits slathered in a thick sausage gravy. Mike and Becky of Pie Pushers in North Carolina staunchly refuse to ever use packaged gravy and try to get ingredients as close to home as possible. "When people are used to eating biscuits and gravy from a truck stop or diner, they have this canned food mentality. When they have one of ours, it changes everything."

BISCUITS

1 ½ lb (680g) self-rising flour, plus more for dusting

1 tbsp (12g) sugar

1 tsp baking powder

½ tsp baking soda

½ lb (227g) butter, diced

2 cups (473ml) buttermilk

COUNTRY SAUSAGE GRAVY

1 lb (453g) local sausage (we prefer Durham's own Firsthand Foods' local country sausage)

1 cup (151g) diced yellow onion

1 tbsp (10g) minced garlic

1 tsp red pepper flakes

1 tsp dried thyme

½ cup (50g) all-purpose flour

3 cups (710ml) whipping cream

Salt and pepper to taste

To make the biscuits, combine the self-rising flour, sugar, baking powder and baking soda in the bowl of a food processor. While the processor is mixing, slowly add the butter until there is an even and coarse consistency.

Transfer the flour and butter mixture to a large mixing bowl and add the buttermilk. With your hands, mix together just until combined. Be careful not to overmix.

Turn out the dough onto a countertop dusted with flour. With a rolling pin, roll the dough out to 1-inch (2.5cm) thickness. With a round biscuit cutter, cut biscuits by applying pressure on the cutter, straight down. Do not twist the cutter while pressing down, which prevents the biscuits from rising properly during the baking process. Place the biscuits on a baking sheet and put in the refrigerator for 15 minutes.

Meanwhile, preheat the oven to 425°F (218°C). Remove the biscuits from the refrigerator and immediately place them into the preheated oven; bake until golden brown, 20 to 30 minutes. Transfer to a cooling rack.

To make the gravy, fry the sausage in a heavy-bottomed pot over medium heat. When the sausage is nearly cooked through, add the onion and cook until translucent.

Stir in the garlic, red pepper flakes and thyme. Cook for 1 to 2 minutes. Add the all-purpose flour and stir well until the clumps are completely gone. You are looking for a pasty, meaty consistency. Let cook for 1 to 2 minutes, stirring occasionally.

Add the cream and reduce the heat to medium-low. Cook until the gravy thickens, 15 to 20 minutes. Remember to stir every couple of minutes to keep the sausage from sticking to the bottom of the pot. Add salt and pepper to taste.

Pour the gravy on top of the hot biscuits and enjoy.

BBQ PULLED PORK TACOS

HILL COUNTRY BARBECUE—JOHN CAPELO—REDWOOD CITY, CA

MAKES 20 TACOS

Sparked by a childhood of weekly cooking sessions with his mom, John's passion is bringing quality Southern barbecue to the Bay Area. He's spent countless hours experimenting with fire, meats, sauces and recipes to ensure his BBQ meets the high standards of the Texas Hill Country from which he hails. "True Texas-style barbecue goes beyond the average barbecue fare to create an art form," he says. "It instills a flavor and tenderness that will never be achieved using the standard grilling method."

PORK RUB

4 tbsp (60g) kosher salt

2 tbsp (24g) granulated sugar

2 tbsp (25g) packed brown sugar

2 tbsp (14g) chili powder

2 tbsp (14g) paprika

1 tbsp (7g) cumin

1 tbsp (10g) minced raw garlic

1 tbsp (9g) minced raw onion

1 tbsp (15g) black pepper

1 tsp cayenne pepper

6-to 8-lb (2.7 to 3.5kg) pork shoulder (we recommend using natural, bone-in pork butt)

SESAME DRESSING

1 cup (236ml) peanut oil

½ cup (118ml) rice wine vinegar

¼ cup (85g) honey

¼ cup (59ml) sesame oil

¼ cup (59ml) soy sauce

3 tbsp (47g) Sriracha sauce

SPICY CILANTRO SESAME SLAW

½ head red cabbage, finely sliced

¼ head green cabbage, finely sliced

2 cups (99g) finely sliced carrot

1 bunch cilantro, chopped

¼ cup (40g) chopped roasted peanuts

Sesame seeds (optional)

**PORKLICIOUS BBQ SAUCE
(SOUTH CAROLINA SWEET MUSTARD)**

1 cup (251g) yellow mustard

½ cup (96g) granulated sugar

¼ cup (50g) packed light brown sugar

¾ cup (177ml) cider vinegar

¼ cup (59ml) apple juice

½ tbsp (4g) chili powder

1 tsp black pepper

1 tsp white pepper

¼ tsp cayenne pepper

½ tsp soy sauce (or omit for gluten-free)

1 tbsp (14g) butter

1 tsp liquid smoke (hickory flavoring)

1 tbsp (15ml) lemon juice

20 (6" [15cm]) flour tortillas

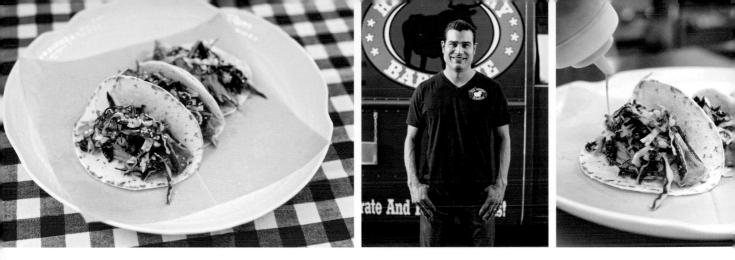

To make the pork rub, combine all the ingredients in a small bowl. Rub all over the pork shoulder.

In your smoker, smoke the pork shoulder at 225°F (107°C) for 12 to 14 hours, or until an internal temperature of 185°F (85°C) is reached. If you do not have a smoker, you may use a smoker box in your barbecue grill with wood chips of your choice. After the pork is done, let it rest for 30 minutes, then pull apart by hand to separate the meat from any unwanted fat and connective tissue. Set aside. Warm just before serving.

While the pork is cooking, prepare the dressing. In a separate sealable container, combine the peanut oil, rice wine vinegar, honey, sesame oil, soy sauce and Sriracha sauce. Cover and shake until the dressing is well mixed.

To make the slaw, in a large bowl, combine the cabbage, carrot and cilantro. Add the dressing a few tablespoons at a time to taste. Just before serving, garnish with the chopped peanuts and sesame seeds.

To make the BBQ sauce, combine the yellow mustard, both sugars, cider vinegar, apple juice, chili powder, black pepper, white pepper and cayenne in a large pot. Simmer for 30 minutes over medium-low heat. Stir in the soy sauce, butter, liquid smoke and lemon juice and simmer for an additional 30 minutes. Let cool and set aside.

Warm the flour tortillas and fill with a layer of pork, then the sauce and the sesame slaw and then finish with more sauce.

ROCKIN' HERO BURGER

MIX'D UP FOOD TRUCK—BRETT EANES—ATLANTA, GA

MAKES 3 BURGERS

A classically trained chef with his own catering company, Brett Eanes was always intrigued by the concept of food trucks. "I decided I'm going to take a classic, and I'm going to have fun with this," he says. "If I get twenty people in line, or if I get two hundred people in line, I'm going to have a ball." The Rockin' Hero is Brett at his most playful, turning a burger into a Mediterranean mouthful. Inspired by his love of gyros, this lamb burger was the one that put his truck on the map.

LAMB PATTIES

1 lb (453g) fresh ground lamb

1 clove garlic, minced

2 oz (57g) dried mint leaves

1 oz (28g) fresh rosemary, finely chopped

Salt and pepper to taste

TZATZIKI SAUCE

1 lb (454g) English cucumbers, peeled and seeded

1 ½ cups (360g) plain Greek yogurt

3 tbsp (45ml) extra-virgin olive oil

1 tbsp (3g) chopped fresh dill

1 clove garlic, crushed

1 tbsp (15g) fresh lemon juice

¼ tsp salt (or more to taste)

Oil, for sautéing

6 slices ciabatta bread

3 to 6 pieces lettuce

3 to 6 slices tomato

3 tbsp (45g) crumbled feta

To make the lamb patties, in a large bowl, combine the lamb, garlic, mint leaves, rosemary and salt and pepper until incorporated. Be careful not to overwork the meat. Wrap in an airtight container and refrigerate for at least 8 hours prior to cooking.

To make the tzatziki sauce, add the cucumbers to a food processor and finely mince, then strain through cheesecloth to remove all the liquid. In a bowl, combine the strained cucumber, Greek yogurt, olive oil, dill, garlic, lemon juice and salt. Mix well, cover and refrigerate for at least 2 hours.

In a pan over medium to high heat, add a touch of oil and the lamb patties and cook to the desired doneness. Panfrying is recommended because char-grilling will mask the aromatics of this fine burger.

Lay 3 slices of the bread on a work surface. Place a burger on each, then top each with a spoonful of tzatziki, 1 or 2 pieces of lettuce, 1 or 2 slices of tomato and 1 tablespoon (15g) of the crumbled feta. Place the remaining slices of bread on top.

PORK BURGER WITH BACON TOMATO JAM

FLAT IRON—TIMOTHY MARK ABELL AND CALEB PATRICO ORTH—LOS ANGELES, CA

MAKES 4 BURGERS

It took Anthony Bourdain's bestseller *Kitchen Confidential* to make Timothy Abell realize he wanted to trade in the pen and papers of his academic life for the pan and spatula of the kitchen. He describes this burger as pork in three dimensions. With a patty made of ground pork and chorizo topped with a bacon tomato jam, it truly is an ode to our piggy friend. "With pork, you can play around and really manipulate the flavor," he explains. "I think it's better than any other burger I've ever had." His Bacon Tomato Jam is also the perfect accompaniment for anything savory.

BACON TOMATO JAM

¼ lb (113g) butter

1 lb (453g) bacon, cut into a large dice

2 medium white onions, cut into a large dice

8 cloves garlic, halved

½ cup (100g) packed brown sugar

1 cup (236g) sherry vinegar

½ cup (118g) sherry wine

2 (12-oz [336g]) cans Italian whole peeled tomatoes

¼ cup (12g) chopped fresh thyme

12 oz (340g) ground pork

6 oz (170g) ground chorizo

1 tbsp (7g) smoked paprika (Spanish is best)

Salt and pepper to taste

4 brioche buns, toasted

4 slices provolone

Handful of arugula

To make the jam, in a large pot over medium heat, add the butter. When the butter foams, add the bacon. Cook for 4 to 5 minutes until the bacon is crispy. Add the onions and garlic and reduce the heat to low heat. Stir frequently until the onions caramelize, about 45 minutes.

Add the sugar and cook for about 5 minutes. The sugar should turn very dark and the contents of the pot should be almost black, but not burned.

Add the sherry vinegar and wine, turn up the heat and stir vigorously. Scrape up anything stuck to the bottom. Cook the sherry for about 1 hour, or until it has reduced to half of its original volume. It should have the consistency of a thick syrup.

Add the tomatoes and thyme and reduce the heat to very low. Cook for at least 4 hours, stirring frequently so the bottom doesn't scorch. It will be a deep red color, like red wine. Set aside to cool. Blend in small batches in a food processor. You now have bacon tomato jam.

In a large mixing bowl, loosely mix the pork, chorizo and smoked paprika. Form into 4 patties. Season both sides with salt and pepper. Grill until the internal temperature is 145°F (63°C) or until the desired doneness. Remove from the grill and let the meat rest for 5 minutes. Serve on a toasted brioche bun with the jam, provolone and arugula.

OXTAIL MAC N' CHEESE

FLAT IRON—TIMOTHY MARK ABELL AND CALEB PATRICK ORTH—LOS ANGELES, CA

SERVES 8 TO 10

If Timothy could describe the Flat Iron Truck with three words, they'd be: American comfort food. "We make things people grew up with and loved, but more refined," he says. "Something your mom made for you, but better." His Oxtail Mac n' Cheese sums up this sentiment perfectly. It's a creamy, thick mac n' cheese that could grace any childhood table, topped with flavorful, red wine–braised oxtail.

4 lb (2kg) oxtails

Salt and pepper

1 onion, chopped

5 cloves garlic, left whole

2 cups (473ml) red wine (we recommend Cabernet Sauvignon)

2 cups (473ml) beer (we recommend Fat Tire)

2 sprigs rosemary

3 cups (709ml) cream

4 tbsp (57g) butter, softened

4 tbsp (25g) all-purpose flour

4 cups (483g) shredded cheese mixture (we use Cheddar, Parmesan, Jack and manchego)

6 cups (1420ml) water

4 cups (463g) dry macaroni

Preheat the oven to 250°F (120°C, or gas mark ½).

Heat a wide, shallow pot over high heat. Season the oxtail with salt and pepper and sear each side for 2 minutes. Remove from the pot. Add the onion and garlic and cook for 5 minutes. Add the wine and beer to deglaze the pan. Put the oxtail and rosemary in a baking dish. Add the onion mixture over the oxtail. Cover the dish and cook for 2 ½ to 3 hours, until the oxtail is tender when pierced with a knife. When the meat is finished, pull it from the pot and shred it while still hot. Reserve the braising liquid for another use.

In a separate pot, bring the cream to a boil. While waiting for the cream to boil, mix the butter and flour in a small bowl with your hands. When the cream is boiling, remove from the heat and add the butter and flour mixture, whisking constantly. The sauce will thicken as you stir. When the sauce is thickened, immediately add the shredded cheese mixture and stir to incorporate. If the sauce is too thick, add cream to thin. Season with salt.

Bring the water to a boil in a medium pot. Add salt. Cook the macaroni following the package directions until al dente. Drain the macaroni and add to the cheese sauce. Serve mac and cheese in bowls topped with the shredded oxtail.

MAKER'S MARK FRIED CHICKEN

BIG D'S GRUB TRUCK—DENNIS KUM—NEW YORK, NY

SERVES 6

Conceived during an epic showdown between seven New York food trucks and seven Boston-based food trucks, this lightly battered, crispy fried chicken took second place in a Maker's Mark Food Truck Bash. The bourbon giant loved it so much that Maker's Mark asked Dennis Kum to run the special longer. "I love whiskey and I love fried chicken," says Dennis. "Anything fried, I'm there." Dennis recommends marinating the chicken for two days for a really intense flavor.

1 cup (236ml) Maker's Mark (or comparable whiskey)

½ cup (118ml) soy sauce

¼ cup (59g) rice wine vinegar

½ cup (100g) packed brown sugar

3 cloves garlic, minced

1 tsp salt

¼ tsp cumin

1 tbsp (21g) honey

2 lb (1kg) chicken thighs

All-purpose flour

Vegetable oil for deep-frying

In a large bowl, combine the whiskey, soy sauce, vinegar, sugar, garlic, salt, cumin and honey. Add the chicken thighs, turn to coat and marinate for one whole day in the refrigerator, two days if you can swing it. If you have the time, it will taste better if you can marinate it for two days.

Remove the chicken from the marinade, discarding the marinade. Spread the flour on a plate and dredge the thighs in the flour.

Pour the oil into a deep pot or tabletop fryer to a depth of 3 to 4 inches (7.5 to 10cm) and heat to 375°F (190°C) on a deep-fat thermometer. Add the chicken in batches and deep-fry for 5 to 10 minutes, until golden brown. If you prefer, you can panfry in less oil. Do not fry too dark because you won't taste much of the bourbon.

CHAPTER 2

PICK IT UP: SANDWICHES

Chandler: You tried to save a sandwich from a bullet?

Joey: I know this doesn't make much sense...

I sometimes feel like Joey from *Friends*. There've been instances when I've eaten a sandwich so amazing that I've looked to the skies and screamed *thank you* at the top of my lungs. Lucky for me, if there's one consistent item you'll see most often on food cart menus, it's some form of sandwich. As a street vendor, it makes sense; you want your customers enjoying your food standing up or sitting down. What better way than putting it between two pieces of bread? But I think there's more to it than that. I often think to myself, maybe people love and appreciate their food so much more when they get to feel it between their fingers. Thank goodness we have sandwiches! Sometimes I feel like it's the best way to enjoy food.

But we're not talking just any kind of sandwich. How many of your lunches consisted of a generic PB&J? Or a plain ham sandwich? You have probably grown tired of eating that same sandwich over and over again. But that's the great thing about this chapter—you have delicious choices now, like American Meltdown's Beer n' Bacon Melt or Doc's of the Bay's Fried Chicken Sandwich with Fennel Slaw. The possibilities are endless!

DOC'S OF THE BAY—ZAK SILVERMAN
OAKLAND, CALIFORNIA

Zak Silverman, founder and owner of Doc's of the Bay, is a devotee of the neighborhood burger joint. The down-home food, the sizzle of the grill, the humble characters seated elbow-to-elbow at the counter: it all speaks to Zak on the same level as warm blankets on a cold day. "There's something about just being able to go to your corner burger establishment and be around a bunch of people and eat a really good, comforting burger that's a priceless experience. It's a uniquely American thing, and something I really love."

It was this love for the quintessential burger shack that led him to start Doc's of the Bay, a food truck determined to radiate the same simple, earnest, feel-good warmth as the neighborhood stands of yesteryear. Named after a well-loved, salt-of-the-earth character in Steinbeck's *Cannery Row*, Doc's specializes in what Zak describes as "thoughtful, high-end comfort food staples on a bun. Just the perfect version of things we'd want to eat every day, with a slight twist."

Zak makes sure every component going into his sandwiches is locally sourced and the highest quality possible. But as serious as he is about his ingredients, his truck has an attitude as playful as it gets. Doc's of the Bay is usually manned by a smiling staff sporting some pretty sweet tuxedo shirts. Their laid-back charm and easy laughs season the food as beautifully as their homemade slaw.

FRIED CHICKEN SANDWICH WITH FENNEL SLAW

DOC'S OF THE BAY—ZAK SILVERMAN—OAKLAND, CA

MAKES 12 SANDWICHES

Zak Silverman adds his own flair to this fried chicken sandwich by incorporating the wonderfully aromatic fennel plant. "We start by brining the chicken, resulting in a final product that is perfectly juicy, salty and a little sweet," he explains. "As the chicken fries, the fennel seed in the breading starts to toast and releases a ton of flavor."

5 boneless, skinless chicken breasts

BRINE
2 qt (2l) water
⅔ cup (128g) granulated sugar
¼ cup (50g) packed brown sugar
⅔ cup (161g) salt
1 tbsp (15g) black pepper
¼ cup (30g) chopped fennel

FENNEL SLAW
1 head green cabbage
1 bulb fresh fennel
3 large carrots
1 bunch of dill

JALAPEÑO BUTTERMILK SLAW DRESSING
3 to 5 jalapeños
1 to 2 cups (220 to 440g) garlic aioli or mayonnaise
1 to 2 cups (236 to 473ml) buttermilk
1 tbsp (15g) black pepper

FOR DREDGING AND FRYING
2 qt (2l) canola oil
½ cup (50g) all-purpose flour
3 tbsp (45g) salt
3 tbsp (45g) black pepper
¼ cup (30g) whole fennel seed
¼ cup (30g) ground fennel seed
3 tbsp (22g) paprika
½ cup (11g) ground cornflakes
3 large eggs
⅓ cup (79ml) water

12 brioche buns

(continued)

FRIED CHICKEN SANDWICH WITH FENNEL SLAW (CONTINUED)

Cut the chicken breasts into sandwich-size pieces.

To make the brine, pour the water into a container large enough to hold the chicken. Add the sugars, salt, black pepper and fennel. Stir the ingredients until the sugars and salt dissolve. Add the chicken and allow to sit overnight in the refrigerator.

To make the slaw, remove the outermost leaves from the green cabbage head, cut out the core and slice it into pieces that will fit into the feeder of a food processor. Use a rotating slicing attachment to shred the cabbage and fennel. If you don't have a food processor or a slicing attachment, slice the cabbage and fennel very thinly with a knife. Switch to a grating attachment for the food processor and shred the carrots. If you don't have a food processor, use a manual grater. Chop the dill roughly and mix all the ingredients together in a large bowl.

To make the dressing, de-seed the jalapeños and puree them in a food processor. If you don't have a food processor, you can use a blender or dice them extremely fine. Stir together equal parts aioli and buttermilk, the pureed jalapeños and the black pepper until combined. Set aside.

Preheat the oven to 300°F (150°C, or gas mark 2) and fill a large pot with frying oil. Heat the oil to 325°F (163°C) on a deep-fat thermometer. Set a cooling rack over a baking sheet

Remove the chicken from the brine and spread out on a parchment-lined baking sheet. Bake the chicken for about 10 minutes. The inside should no longer be pink, but still very moist.

While the chicken cools, set up a breading station. Mix the flour, salt, pepper, both fennel seeds, paprika and cornflakes in a large bowl. Crack the eggs into a second bowl, add the water and scramble the eggs.

Just before frying, dip each piece of chicken thoroughly in the egg mixture. Generously coat the chicken in the flour mixture. Transfer to another bowl for the finished chicken.

Fry the chicken for 1 to 2 minutes, until the crust is golden and crispy and the inside of the chicken is hot.

Just before serving, dress the slaw generously. Load the bottom bun with the slaw, add a piece of chicken and then add a little more dressing on top to the make the top bun stick.

BEER N' BACON MELT

AMERICAN MELTDOWN—PAUL INSERRA—DURHAM, NC

MAKES 4 SANDWICHES

Paul came up with the idea of making melts during evenings spent with friends. In his experience, no one who came over for dinner would ever turn down a freshly made melt. Bread and cheese? What's not to love? In this sandwich, Paul takes it even further by adding two more well-loved ingredients: beer and bacon. The Beer n' Bacon Melt is the culmination of all these ingredients coming together to form a perfect storm of heavenly tastes. "People will travel long distances for this," says Paul. "We've had people tell us they drove from Maryland or Greensboro, North Carolina, just to taste this." We can see why.

RAREBIT

1 tbsp (14g) butter

1 tbsp (6g) all-purpose flour

12-oz (355ml) bottle dark beer (Guinness, stout, porter)

2 tbsp (30ml) Worcestershire sauce

2 tbsp (31g) Dijon mustard

1 tsp Sriracha

1 ½ tbsp (24ml) Frank's RedHot Sauce

1 lb (453g) sharp Cheddar cheese

MELT

12 slices bacon

2 tbsp (29g) butter

8 slices sourdough bread

4 slices Cheddar cheese

Handful sharp arugula

To make the rarebit, over medium heat, add the butter and flour and stir to make a roux. Continue stirring until the roux has thickened and is a blond color. Do not overcook the roux and let it become dark. Add the beer, Worcestershire, mustard, Sriracha and hot sauce in increments and mix well. Start mixing in the cheese and stir constantly. Once all the cheese is mixed in, let the rarebit cool in the refrigerator.

To make the melt, cook the bacon in a skillet over medium heat for 4 to 5 minutes, until crispy and then set aside. Generously butter the outsides of each bread slice. Spread the rarebit on the non-buttered sides, add a slice of cheese and top with a slice of bread, buttered-side up. Once the sandwich is golden and crispy on both sides, open it up and add the arugula and 3 slices of bacon.

THE MATADOR

AMERICAN MELTDOWN—PAUL INSERRA—DURHAM, NC

MAKES 4 SANDWICHES

Paul Inserra has a lifetime of restaurant experience under his belt. Waiting tables and cooking food have been his tickets to independence and travel ever since he was a teen. "I love the adrenaline, organized chaos and frenetic energy of working in a restaurant," he says. Now he has a kitchen he can call his own on the American Meltdown food truck. His main focus is grilled cheese sandwiches. Melty, gooey cheese sandwiched between hot, crusty bread is quite possibly the simplest recipe for pure satisfaction. Paul uses this combination as a springboard for his innovative, surprising melts. The Matador adds a Mediterranean twist to the classic grilled cheese with flavors of roasted bell peppers, almonds and garlic.

ROMESCO SAUCE

6 red bell peppers

1 cup (236ml) olive oil

½ cup (80g) whole cloves garlic

¼ cup (59ml) lemon juice

1 cup (170g) roasted, salted almonds

Salt and pepper to taste

Butter

8 slices sourdough bread

1 cup (120g) grated manchego cheese

Preheat the oven to 475°F (240°C, or gas mark 9). Slice the peppers in half or quarters, discarding the seeds and stems. Place the peppers directly on the rack with a baking sheet underneath to catch the drips and roast until their edges start to blacken, 12 to 15 minutes.

While the peppers are roasting, place the olive oil and garlic into a pot and bring to a simmer over medium-low heat. Cook until the garlic cloves are a light caramel brown, approximately 15 minutes. Remove the garlic and set aside, reserving the oil in the pot.

In a food processor, add the bell peppers, lemon juice, almonds, garlic and ½ cup (120ml) of the olive oil used to cook the garlic and puree. If the mixture is too thick, add more olive oil and lemon juice 1 tablespoon (15ml) at a time. Add salt and pepper to taste.

Butter one side of each slice of bread. Spread the romesco sauce on 4 slices of the bread (non-buttered side) and top with ¼ cup (30g) of the manchego cheese. Top with the remaining slices of bread, buttered-side up. Toast the sandwiches for 2 to 3 minutes on each side in a medium pan over medium heat until each side is golden and crispy.

WHIZ WIT' CLASSIC PHILLY CHEESESTEAK

PHIL'S STEAKS—JIM DREW, J.J. JENSEN, AND KEVIN AND MIA MCCONNELL—NEW YORK, NY

MAKES 1 CHEESESTEAK

Before Kevin, J.J. Jensen and Jim Drew were slinging cheesesteaks from Phil's Steaks, they were in the music industry. Kevin and J.J. toured the world with their own record label before moving to New York and meeting native Philadelphian Jim Drew, also a musician. Jim always pined after the Philly cheesesteaks of his home state, but his searches in local restaurants were forever turning up empty-handed. "We were all having a beer on the roof one night," says Kevin, "and he told us about his idea for opening up a Philly cheesesteak food truck. We started working on it the very next day, and six months later we had our truck on the road." True to their roots, Phil's crew goes as far as to order their ingredients from Philadelphia to perfectly replicate the classic chopped-steak and cheese sandwich. If you want to be really authentic, make sure your cheese is of the neon variety.

8 oz (227g) tenderloin or rib-eye beef

2 tbsp (30ml) canola oil

½ small onion, diced

Salt and pepper to taste

Paprika to taste

2 oz (57g) Cheez Whiz

10" (25cm) Italian hoagie roll

Put the beef in the freezer for 30 minutes to get it really cold before slicing it. Use a mandoline or a very sharp knife to slice the beef very thin.

Heat the canola oil in a small skillet, add the onion and sauté until golden, but do not caramelize, 5 to 10 minutes. Remove the onions from the pan and set aside.

Add the beef to the pan and sprinkle with salt, pepper and a little paprika. Cook the beef for 3 to 4 minutes, or until there is no pink color left. Once done cooking, chop the beef into smaller pieces and mix with the sautéed onions.

Warm the Cheez Whiz over low heat.

Slice open your hoagie roll but do not cut through it. Spread the hot Cheez Whiz liberally on both inside halves of the split hoagie.

In the pan, form the beef and onion mix into the shape of your hoagie roll. Place the hoagie roll Whiz-side down onto the beef and onions mix. Let it sit for 10 seconds.

Take a spatula and slide it under the beef, while holding the hoagie roll in the other hand, and flip it over.

PHILLY STEAK N' EGGS SAMMY

PHIL'S STEAKS—JIM DREW, J.J. JENSEN, AND KEVIN AND MIA MCCONNELL—NEW YORK, NY

MAKES 1 CHEESESTEAK

Originally, Kevin and his crew weren't planning on serving breakfast. But New Yorkers put up some fierce competition when it comes to parking spots. To get the primo spot, Phil's Steaks would hit the street as early as 6 a.m. and figured, instead of waiting around for the lunch crowd, why not turn their classic Philly cheesesteak into a breakfast sandwich by adding eggs? "It may not be the healthiest way to start the day," Kevin admits, "but it's definitely the most delicious way to start the day." Made with chopped, thinly sliced steak, onions, peppers, scrambled eggs and fresh bread, the Philly Steak n' Eggs Sammy is a breakfast sandwich worth waking up for.

4 oz (113g) tenderloin or rib-eye beef

¼ small onion

1 tbsp (15ml) canola oil

Salt and pepper to taste

Paprika to taste

2 eggs

Butter

2 slices white American cheese

6" (15cm) Italian hoagie roll

Put the beef in the freezer for 30 minutes to get it really cold before slicing. Use a mandoline or a very sharp knife to slice the beef very thin.

Dice the onion and sauté in a skillet with canola oil for 5 to 10 minutes, until golden, but do not caramelize the onions. Remove the onions from the pan and set aside.

Add the beef to the pan and sprinkle with salt, pepper and a little paprika. Cook the beef for 3 to 4 minutes, or until there is no pink color left. Once done cooking, chop the beef into smaller pieces and mix with the sautéed onions. Remove from the heat and set aside.

Scramble the eggs with a little butter. Add the beef and onion mix to the scrambled eggs and mix together. In the pan, form the beef, onions and eggs mixture into the shape of your hoagie roll. Lay the cheese slices on top of the mixture, allowing them to melt completely. Place your hoagie roll over the mixture for 10 seconds.

Take a spatula and slide it under the beef, while holding the hoagie roll in the other hand, and flip it over.

GRILLED CHICKEN CORDON BLEU SLIDERS

NOLA GIRL FOOD TRUCK AND CATERING—DANNIELLE JUDIE—NEW ORLEANS, LA

MAKES 16 SLIDERS

"Chicken Cordon Bleu is one of those forgotten dishes," Dannielle Judie reminisces. "When that style first came out everyone ate it, but now you don't see it as much anymore." Which is a shame because we feel the combination of thin-sliced ham, juicy chicken and melted Gruyère cheese is more than enough to earn the title "Cordon Bleu" or "Blue Ribbon." Luckily, Dannielle is around to revive and update this classic recipe by making it into sliders and adding a touch of Louisiana with a piquant Creole aioli.

CREOLE MUSTARD AIOLI

½ cup (125g) Creole mustard or spicy mustard

½ cup (110g) mayonnaise

2 tbsp (30ml) olive oil

1 tbsp (15ml) fresh lemon juice

2 cloves garlic, minced or grated

¼ tsp Creole seasonings

¼ tsp cayenne pepper

1 cup (235ml) Worcestershire sauce

2 tbsp (30ml) olive oil

1 tbsp (15g) kosher salt

1 tsp black pepper

½ tsp cayenne pepper

1 tsp cumin

1 tsp garlic powder

1 tsp onion powder

4 boneless, skinless whole chicken breasts

16 slices premium deli ham

16 slices Swiss or Gruyère cheese

16 Hawaiian rolls, mini buns or slider buns

To make the aioli, in a medium bowl, add all the ingredients and whisk together until well incorporated. Cover and refrigerate for 30 minutes to 1 hour before using.

In a large bowl, add the Worcestershire sauce, olive oil, salt, black pepper, cayenne pepper, cumin, garlic powder and onion powder. Whisk vigorously until all the ingredients are well blended to make a marinade.

Split the chicken breasts in half and rinse. Add the chicken to the marinade, cover and marinate for at least 30 minutes. Drain the chicken and discard the marinade.

Apply nonstick spray on a rectangular grill pan or grill pan skillet and heat over medium-high heat. When the pan begins to lightly smoke, place the chicken on the hot grill pan, being careful not to crowd the meat. After about 5 minutes of searing, the meat will show dark grill marks. Turn the chicken over to the other side and repeat.

After about 3 minutes of cooking, place the ham slices over the chicken, followed by the cheese slices on top of the ham. Continue to cook for about 3 minutes, until the cheese is melted. Make sure the chicken is fully cooked before serving.

Warm the sliced buns on a griddle or pan until toasty. Spread the Creole mustard aioli on the top bun. Cut the chicken in half to fit and place on the bottom bun. Top the chicken with more aioli.

YOLKO ONO

FRIED EGG I'M IN LOVE—JACE KRAUSE—PORTLAND, OR

MAKES 6 SANDWICHES

Fried Egg I'm in Love is known for serving up playfully named, blue collar, egg-centric breakfast sandwiches to Portland, Oregon, city dwellers. Former bandmates Jace Krause and Ryan Lynch both left corporate careers to dream up ever-innovative sandwiches to brighten any morning. Made with pesto and homemade sausage, the Yolko Ono is one of their signature items. And don't worry, this sandwich won't be breaking up their food cart team anytime soon.

PESTO

1 cup (44g) basil leaves, rinsed and dried

½ cup (90g) shredded Parmesan cheese

⅓ cup (80ml) extra-virgin olive oil

¼ cup (31g) pine nuts

1 tbsp (10g) minced garlic

½ tsp sea salt

Pinch of black pepper

SAUSAGE

⅓ yellow onion

1 tsp yellow mustard

1 tsp paprika

1 tsp minced garlic

Pinch of sea salt

Pinch of dried oregano

Pinch of black pepper

1 lb (454g) raw ground pork sausage

1 to 2 tbsp (14 to 28g) butter

6 slices fresh sourdough bread (use a large, wide loaf)

¾ cup (75g) Parmesan cheese

6 eggs

Pinch of black pepper

Pinch of cayenne

To make the pesto, pack the basil in a food processor, then add the Parmesan, olive oil, pine nuts, garlic, salt and pepper. Let the ingredients blend for 30 to 45 seconds, then scrape any bits from the side and blend for another 30 seconds. Let it rest for a minute, and then blend again for another 30 seconds, until smooth.

To make the sausage, puree the onion in a small food processor and place in a bowl. Add all the ingredients, except the sausage, and stir until blended. Put the sausage in a large mixing bowl and break it up into small pieces. Then add the onion puree and use your hands to blend the mix into the sausage. The puree should be blended evenly with the sausage and you should see no clumps. Form the sausage into balls and place on a dinner plate or small baking pan. You should be able to form 6 balls, slightly bigger than a golf ball. Be sure to roll and form the balls tightly.

Place a cast-iron griddle or large pan over medium heat. Melt the butter in a small dish in the microwave. Use a basting brush to spread the butter down the center of the bread slices. Place the buttered-side down on the griddle. Add a heaping tablespoon (15g) of the pesto to the bread and use a spatula to spread the pesto to evenly cover all the bread, right up to the edges. Sprinkle as much Parmesan as you desire on top of the pesto. At the cart, we typically use about 2 tablespoons (12.5g) on each sandwich.

Take a sausage ball and place on the griddle or a separate large pan. Use a strong metal spatula to press the ball into a patty. You will be covering one half of the bread with this patty, so match the patty size to the bread.

Use your basting brush to spread a thin layer of butter on the griddle, and crack the egg on it. Sprinkle a small pinch of black pepper and cayenne on the egg.

Check the sausage patty and cook for 3 to 4 minutes on each side, until it has char on it. When the whites of the egg start turning opaque, flip the egg. Let the sausage and egg cook for about 2 minutes after flipping. Then place the sausage on one half of the bread and top it with the egg. Use a knife to cut the bread in half and fold it over to create a sandwich. Your bread should have a nice brown toasted mark down the center.

PORCHETTA SANDWICH WITH PIMENTO CHEESE

PORCHETTA—CHEFS MATTHEW HAYDEN AND NICHOLAS CROSSON—DURHAM, NC

MAKES 12 TO 14

North Carolinians know their pork. Nicholas Crosson wanted to find a way to give his customers the meat they crave without being just another barbecue joint. Having traveled in his youth, Nicholas fell in love with Mediterranean flavors and knew the Italian tradition of slow-roasting an herb-stuffed pork loin would be a hit. He was right. His pork-centric food truck Porchetta serves up delicious sandwiches to a loyal following. This recipe combines tender, moist porchetta with a fantastically zesty pimento cheese spread.

PORCHETTA

3 tbsp (45g) black pepper, freshly ground

3 tbsp (23g) fennel seed, freshly ground

¼ cup (60g) kosher salt

6 lb (3kg) boneless pork Boston butt

½ cup (10g) chopped fresh rosemary

½ cup (10g) chopped fresh sage

¼ cup (10g) chopped fresh thyme

¼ cup (40g) chopped garlic

PIMENTO CHEESE SPREAD

8 oz (227g) cream cheese

16 oz (454g) sharp Cheddar cheese

3 tbsp (22g) smoked paprika

½ cup (85g) chopped roasted pimentos or roasted red peppers

3 tbsp (45ml) Frank's RedHot Sauce

¼ cup (55g) mayonnaise

3 cloves garlic, minced

1 tsp Worcestershire sauce

28 slices ciabatta bread, 2 slices per sandwich

14 oz (392g) sautéed onions

1 ¾ cups (415ml) canola oil

To make the porchetta, rub the black pepper, fennel seed and salt onto the pork. Cover and let rest overnight in the refrigerator.

Preheat the oven to 350°F (180°C, or gas mark 4). Mix the rosemary, sage, thyme and garlic together in a small bowl and rub it into the pork. Place the pork into a deep roasting pan and add any excess herbs to the pan. Cover with foil and place in the oven for 4 hours, or until the internal temperature reaches 170°F (77°C). Turn down the oven temperature to 250°F (120°C, or gas mark ½) and cook for 30 minutes. Remove from the oven and allow to rest for 1 hour in the liquid that has rendered out.

To make the pimento cheese spread, combine the cream cheese, sharp Cheddar cheese, paprika, roasted pimentos, hot sauce, mayonnaise, garlic and Worcestershire sauce in a stand mixer with a paddle attachment. Mix on medium speed until all the ingredients are evenly incorporated.

Slice the porchetta and place a generous amount on one slice of the ciabatta. Top with the sautéed onions. Add an even layer of pimento cheese on the other slice of ciabatta.

Heat a nonstick skillet over medium-low heat, add 2 tablespoons (30ml) canola oil, place the sandwich in the pan and cook for 2 to 3 minutes on each side, until golden brown.

SMOKED PORK LOIN SANDWICH ON ROSEMARY FOCACCIA

RUE CHOW—JARETT AND RACHEL EYMARD—NEW ORLEANS, LA

MAKES 4 TO 6 SANDWICHES

The Smoked Pork Loin Sandwich is near and dear to Rachel Eymard's heart, calling to mind weekends in the backyard with dad. "We often spent Sundays around his barbecue pit," she recalls. "His pork loin was always amazing. We decided to take that inspiration and season it with Italian herbs, fresh rosemary and garlic and smoke it." The result is a tender, perfectly seasoned loin that complements a homemade rosemary focaccia. "The rosemary bread is just a simple bread to make, but it's delicious. We take that bread and toast it with olive oil until it's a little crunchy, then put this pork loin on it with a Creole mayo. It's just dynamite."

ROSEMARY FOCACCIA

2 ¼ tsp (7g) rapid-rise yeast

8 tsp (32g) sugar

2 tsp (10g) salt

3 cups (710ml) warm water

6 ¼ cups (621g) all-purpose flour

¼ cup (60ml) olive oil

2 tbsp (5g) chopped fresh rosemary

Salt and pepper to taste

SMOKED PORK LOIN

¼ tsp red pepper flakes

1 tsp Italian herbs

Salt and pepper to taste

1 lb (454g) pork loin

CREOLE MAYONNAISE

½ cup (110g) mayonnaise

¼ cup (63g) Creole mustard

2 tbsp (29g) melted butter

½ bunch scallions, minced

2 tbsp (28g) butter

1 sweet onion, sliced and grilled

1 cup (341g) mixed greens

To make the focaccia, mix the yeast, sugar, salt and water in a large bowl with a whisk and allow it to sit for 5 to 10 minutes. Add the flour and mix well. Put the dough in a lightly oiled bowl and let it rise until it doubles in size, about 40 minutes.

Lightly oil a half-sheet pan and spread the dough out in the pan. Gently press your fingers into the dough to make divots throughout. Let the dough rise again for 40 minutes, until it doubles in size.

Preheat the oven to 450°F (230°C, or gas mark 8). Brush the dough with the olive oil, and sprinkle with the rosemary, salt and pepper, in that order. Bake for 15 minutes, until golden brown.

To make the pork loin, combine the red pepper flakes, herbs, and salt and pepper in a small bowl. Rub all over the pork loin. Char-grill the pork loin over high heat to achieve nice grill marks. When the smoker has reached 250°F (121°C), add the pork and cook for about 3 ½ hours or until the internal temperature is 155°F (68°C). Remove from the smoker and let cool.

To make the mayonnaise, mix the mayonnaise, Creole mustard, butter and scallions in a bowl and set aside.

Slice the bread into squares and split it down the middle. In a hot skillet, melt the butter. Add the bread and toast for 1 to 2 minutes, or until golden brown. Put a generous portion of the Creole mayonnaise on both sides of the bread. Thinly slice the pork loin and put 4 or 5 slices on the sandwich, then add the grilled onion and mixed greens.

CRISPY MEATLOAF SLIDERS

WHIPOUT!—BRETT DOWNEY—EMERYVILLE, CA

MAKES 10 SLIDERS

WhipOut! is American comfort food done the high-end artisanal way. A self-proclaimed perfectionist, Rob John hired chef Brett Downey to meet his high standards. The Crispy Meatloaf Slider takes a Norman Rockwellian dish—meatloaf—breads it, fries it and serves it with a garlic aioli and onion jam. Everything from the ketchup to the pickles is made from scratch!

DILL PICKLES

2 lb (907g) pickling cucumbers with thin skins

4 tsp (20g) salt

3 cups (710ml) white wine vinegar

2 cups (383g) granulated sugar

½ cup (118ml) water

1 head garlic, halved horizontally

1 bunch of fresh dill

1 tsp dill seeds

KETCHUP

1 large white or yellow onion, diced small

2 tbsp (30ml) oil

4 cloves garlic, minced

1 (28-oz [794g]) can whole peeled tomatoes

1 tbsp (3g) chopped fresh thyme

2 cups (473ml) apple cider vinegar

2 cups (383g) granulated sugar

4 bay leaves

2 tbsp (14g) mustard powder

2 tbsp (30g) finely ground black pepper

2 tbsp (12g) finely ground allspice

Kosher salt to taste

FLAVOR BASE

4 oz (113g) ground (or finely chopped) bacon

1 small onion, finely diced

1 stalk celery, finely diced

1 large carrot, finely diced

2 tbsp (30ml) Worcestershire sauce

2 tbsp (25g) packed brown sugar

1 cup (251g) ketchup

1 tbsp (15g) finely ground pepper

1 tbsp (3g) chopped fresh thyme

1 tbsp (15g) kosher salt

To make the dill pickles, slice the cucumbers to the desired thickness. In a large bowl, toss the sliced cucumbers in 1 teaspoon of the salt and allow to rest for at least 1 hour in the fridge. Drain thoroughly and place in a heatproof bowl. In a large pot over high heat, whisk together the vinegar, sugar, water, garlic, fresh dill, dill seeds and the remaining 1 tablespoon (15g) salt. When the brine comes to a boil, pour over the sliced cucumbers. Allow to sit overnight before packaging into a sealed container. Keeps for 3 to 4 weeks.

To make the ketchup, caramelize the onion with the oil in a large stockpot over medium heat for 15 to 20 minutes. Lower the heat, add the garlic and stir for 30 seconds. Add the tomatoes, thyme apple cider vinegar, sugar, bay leaves, mustard powder, black pepper, allspice and kosher salt. Simmer for 4 to 5 hours, stirring occasionally. Remove from the heat and cool completely. Blend the ketchup in small batches in a food processor until it becomes smooth. Add salt to taste.

To make the flavor base, brown the bacon in a large heavy-bottomed stockpot. After the bacon is browned and there's a good amount of fat, lower the heat, remove the bacon and reserve the fat. Add the onion, celery and carrot to the fat and cook until softened, 10 to 15 minutes. Add the bacon and Worcestershire, brown sugar, ketchup, pepper, thyme and salt and simmer for 30 minutes, until thickened. Remove from the heat and cool thoroughly.

To make the garlic aioli, coarsely chop the garlic and blend in a food processor or blender until it becomes a fine paste. Add the egg yolks, lemon juice, salt and Dijon mustard. Continue to blend slowly until it is light in color and frothy. Slowly drizzle in the oil in a thin stream. If the mixture gets too thick and does not form a smooth sauce, add the water. Blend until all the vegetable oil is incorporated. Set aside until ready to use.

GARLIC AIOLI

1 head garlic, cloves separated and peeled

2 egg yolks

Juice of 1 lemon

1 tsp salt

1 tsp Dijon mustard

3 cups (710ml) vegetable oil

2 tbsp (30ml) cold water

ONION JAM

2 tbsp (30ml) vegetable oil

5 large white or yellow onions, thinly sliced

Splash of apple cider vinegar

2 tbsp (24g) granulated sugar

2 tbsp (30ml) Worcestershire sauce

Kosher salt and freshly ground pepper

MEAT MIXTURE

2 lb (907g) ground beef

3 eggs

2 cups (241g) fine bread crumbs

1 tbsp (10g) minced garlic

2 tbsp (30ml) Worcestershire sauce

1 tbsp (15g) kosher salt

2 tsp (10g) finely ground pepper

BREADING

2 cups (199g) all-purpose flour

6 eggs beaten with 1 cup (236ml) water

2 cups (241g) panko bread crumbs

6 cups (1410ml) canola oil

10 small French rolls, split and toasted

To make the onion jam, add the oil and onions to a very hot, heavy-bottomed pot. As the onions wilt and release their water, stir occasionally. When all the liquid is evaporated and the onions are like tar and dark, 30 to 45 minutes, add the vinegar, sugar and Worcestershire. Stir in salt and pepper to taste. Set aside until ready to assemble. Preheat the oven to 375°F (190°C, or gas mark 5).

To make the meat mixture, combine all the ingredients very thoroughly in a bowl set over another bowl of ice to keep the mixture cold. Add the cold flavor base and continue to mix until completely incorporated.

Lay out a 2-foot (61cm) sheet of aluminum foil, and on top of that a 2-foot (61cm) sheet of ovenproof parchment paper. Form the meatloaf into a log, and place lengthwise on the bottom quarter of the sheets of foil and parchment. Carefully roll the log, making sure to snugly wrap the meatloaf, not leaving any air pockets. Pinch the ends at the edges of the log, and twist tightly to form a uniform log. Place on a rack on top of a sheet pan to catch the drippings.

Bake for 1 ½ hours, or until a thermometer inserted into the middle of the log reads 165°F (74°C). Cool the log in an ice bath and slice into disks 1-inch (2.5cm) thick.

To make the breading station, in 3 separate pans, lay out the flour, beaten eggs and water and panko. First, coat the disks in the flour, then the egg and finally in the panko. Lay the finished meatloaf disks on a tray until ready to fry.

Pour the oil into a deep pot or fryer to a depth of 4 to 5 inches (10 to 15cm) and bring to 350°F (177°C) on a deep-fat thermometer. Fry the meatloaves for 5 minutes, until golden and crispy on the outside.

Assemble the sliders with the fried meatloaf, garlic aioli, ketchup, onion jam and a slice of dill pickle on each roll.

CRAB A HOLD OF ME

MELTS MY HEART—WES ISIP—SAN JOSE, CA

MAKES 1 SANDWICH

Owner Brian Aflague's love of grilled cheese came from homemade childhood meals in his grandfather's kitchen. It was a nostalgic meal that never quite gave up its spot as his #1 favorite food. At Melts My Heart, Brian pays tribute to the classic grilled cheese by constantly looking for new ways to offer up the cheese-and-bread combo. His favorite place of inspiration is his own crew, often putting their ideas into practice and creating instant favorites. One such favorite is the signature crab melt made with fresh crab, mild Cheddar cheese and a touch of Old Bay seasoning.

1 (16-oz [454g]) can premium quality super or jumbo lump crabmeat (not imitation)

1 stalk celery, diced

¼ red onion, diced

1 scallion, chopped

Old Bay seasoning to taste

Black pepper to taste

2 to 3 tbsp (28 to 41g) mayonnaise

Butter

2 slices of fresh sourdough bread

3 slices of mild Cheddar cheese

2 slices of tomatoes

Combine the crab, celery, red onion, scallion, Old Bay and black pepper in a small bowl and mix thoroughly. Add the mayonnaise and mix thoroughly again.

Place a skillet over medium-high heat. Butter one side of each slice of bread. Place both slices of bread buttered-side down onto the skillet. Add the cheese to both slices of bread. Scoop 4 ounces (112g) of the crab mix on top of the cheese on one slice of bread.

Place 2 slices of tomatoes directly on the pan and grill for a few seconds on each side. Place the tomatoes on the other slice of bread and toast for 3 minutes. Flip the slice of bread with the tomatoes onto the other slice of bread with the crab mix. Press down firmly and toast both sides for 2 to 3 minutes, until golden brown and crispy.

SAM'S FAMOUS LOBSTER ROLL

SAM'S CHOWDERMOBILE—LEWIS ROSSMAN—HALF MOON BAY, CA

MAKES 4 LOBSTER ROLLS

The origin story behind Sam's ChowderMobile is different from most food trucks in that it started out as a single restaurant, Sam's Chowder House. "The restaurant got so busy. My partner and I would sit in the office late at night and ask, 'How can we reach more people?'" The idea of a mobile truck version took hold. The secret to their popularity? It's all about the lobster. Lewis Rossman believes there are some ingredients so flavorful and perfect on their own that all you can hope to do is showcase them in the manner they deserve. Combine them with too many other ingredients, and you risk drowning out that perfect note. "We're not really into cloying flavors or mayonnaises," says Lewis about their signature lobster roll. "It's all about really fresh-tasting, moist lobster in its purest form with melted butter. That, for me, is really the best." Sam's ChowderMobile serves its lobster rolls "naked": fresh knuckle and claw meat with melted butter and a little bit of celery served on an artisan roll.

2 whole 1 ½-lb (680g) lobsters

½ cup (113g) butter, melted

4 brioche hot dog buns, sides trimmed

⅓ cup (60g) chopped celery

Bring a large pot of water to a boil and steam the lobsters for 12 minutes. Remove and cool the lobsters, and then remove all of the meat. Chop the meat into generous chunks and set aside.

Heat a sauté pan with 2 tablespoons (28g) of the butter and toast the sides of the buns. Remove the buns when they are light brown on both sides.

Add the remaining 6 tablespoons (84g) of butter, the celery and the lobster meat to the pan. Heat gently until warmed through, 1 to 2 minutes. Be careful not to overcook the mixture, or the meat will lose its moisture.

Divide the meat into 4 servings and stuff the buns with it.

BIG-ASS ROAST BEEF SANDWICH WITH BÉCHAMEL CHEESE SAUCE

BIG-ASS SANDWICHES—BRIAN WOOD—PORTLAND, OR

MAKES 15 TO 20 SANDWICHES

This is one sandwich worthy of its name. Husband-and-wife team Brian and Lisa Wood are known for seriously piling on the ingredients at their food cart Big-Ass Sandwiches. Their roast beef sandwich combines a tender chuck roast, homemade béchamel sauce and French fries. (That's right, French fries right on the sandwich!) It's one sandwich that would make Dagwood weep.

ROAST BEEF

5 lb (2.3kg) chuck roast

3 tbsp (45g) salt

3 tbsp (45g) pepper

3 tbsp (22g) onion powder

3 tbsp (22g) garlic powder

BÉCHAMEL CHEESE SAUCE

1 cup (99g) all-purpose flour

½ cup (113g) butter

2 qt (1.9l) milk

2 ½ lb (1.1kg) Tillamook Cheddar cheese, shredded

Pinch of sea salt and freshly ground pepper

FRENCH FRIES

15 russet potatoes

6 cups (1410ml) vegetable oil

Sea salt to taste

15 to 20 ciabatta rolls

To make the roast beef, preheat the oven to 225°F (107°C, or gas mark ¼). Season the chuck roast with salt, pepper, onion powder and garlic powder. Place in a roasting pan and cook the beef for 45 minutes to 1 hour, until it reaches an internal temperature of 120°F (49°C). Let it cool for 24 hours. When ready to serve, thinly slice 4 ounces (112g) of the roast beef per sandwich and grill to a final temperature of 145°F (63°C).

To make the béchamel cheese sauce, stir together the flour and butter in a saucepan over low heat. Add the milk and stir until you have a smooth consistency. Add the cheese and stir constantly for approximately 40 minutes, until you have a velvety fondue consistency. Add a pinch of sea salt and black pepper to taste.

To make the fries, hand cut the potatoes into fries ¼ inch (6mm) thick. Pour the oil into a deep pot or fryer to a depth of 4 to 5 inches (10 to 15cm) and heat to 350°F (177°C) on a deep-fat thermometer. Add the fries in batches and cook until three-fourths of the way done; strain from the oil and cool. Reserve the oil in the pot, adding more to reach the same level as needed.

When ready to assemble the sandwiches, bring the oil back to temperature and fry the French fries again until cooked to your preferred crispness, strain and season with salt to taste.

Slice a ciabatta roll down one side like a clamshell. Place 4 ounces (113g) of roast beef on the bottom of the bread and top with a handful of fries. Pour ½ cup (120ml) of béchamel cheese sauce over the fries, add a few more fries and roll everything up in sandwich paper.

CHAPTER 3

SPOONFULS: SOUPS AND CHILIES

My family was one of those families who ate dinner together every night at 6 p.m. sharp and my mom always prepared homemade soup. At diners when they ask me whether I want soup or salad, I always say soup. It's something that always makes me feel nourished and energized in a magical way. I don't think we eat enough soup nowadays; it seems to be more and more of an afterthought or something we eat only when we're sick. But maybe the recipes in this chapter will change your mind.

Whether you start your meal with a bowl of soup or make it your meal, soup is a great way to get lots of concentrated flavors of your favorite vegetables or proteins. There's a transformative quality to soup. Healthy things you may not like take on a different quality in soup form. When's the last time you ate a split pea? But make it as a soup and I bet you'll take seconds and thirds!

You're probably wondering whether there are carts that devote themselves to just soups and chilies. For you chili fans out there (meaning everyone), LA's Chili Philosopher specializes in just chili. For those wintry days serving outdoors, their Spanish Chili sounds perfect, as does Deli-icous's Watermelon Gazpacho for those humid New York summers. See, there really is a food cart for everything imaginable.

SAVOR SOUP HOUSE—ADAM DUNN AND COLLEEN SCHROHT

PORTLAND, OREGON

There's a classic episode of *Portlandia* where Fred and Carrie's characters become obsessed with the personal profile of a chicken on which they're about to dine. They grill their waitress, "What was his name?" "Was he happy?" "Did he have a lot of friends?" "Did he have hobbies?" Their waitress is only too happy to oblige, providing a dossier detailing the life history and interests of said chicken.

While the scene is clearly a satire of Portland's increasing mania for all things local and homegrown, this is becoming one of our favorite characteristics of Pacific Northwest cuisine. Because most of America browses Technicolor fruits and plastic-wrapped slabs of meat in boxy, air-conditioned supermarkets, we tend to forget where our food comes from. It's why we're grateful for people like Adam Dunn and Colleen Schroht, owners of Savor Soup House in downtown Portland, Oregon.

As Adam puts it, "The mindfulness of your ingredients goes a long way." There is no lack of mindfulness in Adam and Colleen's kitchen. Both chefs are heavily involved in the agricultural process of everything that goes into their delicious soups. They've spearheaded a volunteer program to oversee crop rotation at local farms and have spent the last few years raising their own pigs. Colleen grew up on a farm raising pigs, and her expertise is instrumental in Savor Soup House upholding a farm-to-spoon model. All this love and hard work shines through in their soups, where local, seasonal ingredients are clearly the stars. Fred and Carrie would definitely approve.

SIMPLY CAULIFLOWER

SAVOR SOUP HOUSE—ADAM DUNN AND COLLEEN SCHROHT—PORTLAND, OR

SERVES 4

"Some of our bestsellers are the really simple ones. We've definitely found that using from-scratch stock really makes the soup," says Adam. One of his favorites is the Simply Cauliflower soup. "It's super simple," he says. "It's not super attractive on a menu, but it's one we pass out all the time and everyone's surprised by how delicious it is."

1 large head cauliflower, trimmed
1 large yellow onion, diced
2 tbsp (30ml) olive oil
6 cloves garlic
1 ½ qt (1420ml) vegetable stock
Salt and pepper to taste
Extra-virgin olive oil, for drizzling

Remove the core and leaves from the cauliflower and chop into large chunks.

In a pot, sauté the onion in the olive oil over medium-high heat until translucent, 4 to 5 minutes. Add the garlic, turn down the heat to medium and sauté for 30 seconds. Next, add the vegetable stock and bring to a boil over medium-high heat. Add the cauliflower to the pot and cook for at least 30 minutes, until it has completely softened.

In a blender, puree the soup in batches until smooth, being careful to hold the lid with a pot holder. Season with salt and pepper to taste. Ladle into bowls. Top with cracked pepper and drizzle with extra-virgin olive oil.

SAVOR
soup house

BUTTERNUT SQUASH AND APPLE BISQUE

SAVOR SOUP HOUSE—ADAM DUNN AND COLLEEN SCHROHT—PORTLAND, OR

SERVES 5

On a cold winter day, nothing can spread that warm glow like a good bowl of soup. "This is a super simple comfort food that's nice to come home to," says Adam Dunn. "It can be made relatively quickly, and it's a great way to relax and warm up." Rich, creamy butternut squash is brightened up by sweet apple butter and citrus zest.

1 large butternut squash

Olive oil, for coating

Water

1 large yellow onion, diced

4 tbsp (56g) butter

1 ½ qt (1420ml) vegetable stock

8 oz (227g) apple butter

¼ cup (61g) cream

2 tbsp (25g) packed brown sugar

Zest and juice of 1 lemon, or to taste

Zest and juice of 1 orange, or to taste

Salt and pepper to taste

Preheat the oven to 375°F (190°C, or gas mark 5). Halve and seed the butternut squash and place skin-side up on a baking pan. Coat the squash lightly with olive oil, add a dash of water to the pan and bake for 45 minutes; this helps separate the skin of the squash for easy peeling.

Sauté the diced onion in the butter in a medium pot over medium heat. Add the vegetable stock and apple butter and bring to a boil over medium-high heat.

Once the squash is done, scoop out the flesh and add it to a blender along with the onion mixture, cream, sugar, lemon and orange zests, salt and pepper. Add the lemon and orange juices to taste. Blend until all the ingredients are thoroughly smooth.

SEAFOOD SOUP

FISHEY BIZNESS SEAFOOD CO.—DENNIS WHITE—AUSTIN, TX

SERVES 6 TO 8

Dennis White sees cooking first and foremost as an expression of creativity, of taking something you like and finding a way to improve upon it. "Everything you do as a cook is pretty personal." The son of a shrimper of thirty-five years, Dennis spent weeks as a kid on a shrimp boat eating a fish soup made by the crew. This Seafood Soup is Dennis's way of infusing the traditional Texas Caldo soup with a bit of his own history.

6 cups (1420ml) water

5 tbsp (75ml) tomato soup

¼ cup (60g) shrimp base or 3 cubes shrimp bouillon

3 carrots, sliced

½ onion, diced

2 potatoes, cubed

2 stalks celery, sliced

2 tbsp (30g) salt

2 tbsp (30g) garlic powder

2 tbsp (30g) onion powder

2 tbsp (30g) black pepper

2 tbsp (30g) Cajun seasoning

2 tbsp (30g) tomato bouillon

1 lb (454g) shrimp, peeled and deveined

2 large fish fillets

In a large pot, add all the ingredients except for the shrimp and fish. Cook the potatoes and carrots for about 1 hour, until they become soft and tender. Once they have softened, add the shrimp and fish and cook for another 30 to 45 minutes.

WATERMELON GAZPACHO

DELI-ICIOUS—SUSAN TOWER—RALEIGH, NC

SERVES 8

Before Susan Tower even thought of mixing the ingredients for her first food truck dish, she was mixing sounds as an audio engineer for some pretty big acts (think David Copperfield or Anthrax). When the hectic travel of touring began to take its toll, Susan decided to take a breather and settle down in Albany, New York. There, she worked at a small bakery where she learned an appreciation for the art of making food from scratch. Now Susan serves a lot of people on the go from her North Carolina food truck, but she doesn't think taste and wholesomeness should be sacrificed for ease and convenience. She's a firm believer that simple, fresh ingredients should speak for themselves. "I love this Watermelon Gazpacho," she says. "Sometimes I just put it in a jug and drink it throughout the day. Someone once said the watermelon gazpacho is a garden in your mouth."

8 cups (1400g) chopped seedless watermelon

1 English cucumber, peeled, seeded and diced

1 red bell pepper, cored, seeded and finely diced

1 jalapeño, seeded and finely diced

1 shallot, minced

¼ cup (10g) chopped fresh basil

¼ cup (10g) chopped fresh mint leaves

3 tbsp (44ml) red wine vinegar

2 tbsp (278ml) extra-virgin olive oil

¾ tsp salt (optional)

Sour cream, for serving

Pesto (page 222), for serving

Mix all the ingredients in a large mixing bowl. Reserve 3 cups (750g) and puree the rest of the mixture with an immersion blender or countertop blender until you have reached the desired consistency. Mix in the reserved diced mixture. Top the soup with sour cream or my favorite, a drizzle of pesto (see page 222 for Frencheeze's Homemade Basil Pesto)!

SPANISH PORK SHOULDER CHILI

THE CHILI PHILOSOPHER—ALEX KAVALLIEROU—LOS ANGELES, CA

SERVE 4 TO 6

One of the things we love about food trucks is the emphasis on doing one thing and doing it well. Alex Kavallierou came to this same conclusion when considering opening up his own food truck in Los Angeles. "You can have one item, serve one thing, from a food truck, and that's okay." Alex's one item is chili—that spicy, simmering, meat and bean stew. Alex uses pork shoulder, Spanish chorizo (not to be confused with Mexican chorizo) and white beans for a Spanish *fabada*-inspired chili.

---

2 tsp (9g) corn oil

1 ½ lb (680g) pork shoulder, cut into 1 ½" (3.8cm) pieces

5 ½ oz (156g) dry-cured Spanish chorizo

1 yellow onion, diced

1 red bell pepper or red Anaheim pepper, cored, seeded, and diced

1 ½ tsp (4g) paprika (Spanish or Hungarian)

1 tbsp (12g) sugar

1 (750ml) bottle white wine or cider

½ tsp red pepper flakes

Water

4 cloves garlic, finely chopped

1 (14-oz [92g]) can Great Northern beans or cannelloni beans, drained

Salt and black pepper to taste

White vinegar to taste

2 to 3 tbsp (5 to 8g) chopped fresh parsley

Heat the oil in a large pot or Dutch oven over high heat. Brown the pork shoulder for 5 minutes on each side and set aside. In the same pot, fry the Spanish chorizo until it starts to brown and the oil turns a light orange. Set aside the chorizo with the pork.

Turn down the heat to medium-high. Cook the onion and pepper in the pot until they turn translucent, 5 to 6 minutes. Add the paprika, sugar and wine and simmer for 20 minutes, until the wine has reduced by a third.

Add the red pepper flakes, pork, chorizo and garlic and add water to cover. Put the lid on and cook for about 30 minutes. Add the beans and cook for another 30 minutes, or until the pork is tender. Do not overcook to where the pork disintegrates. Add the salt, pepper and white vinegar to taste.

Garnish each serving liberally with the parsley. Serve with crusty bread.

BEEF AND BACON CHILI WITH CORN BREAD WAFFLES

WAFFLE AMORE—JUDY VANDOORNE—SAN JOSE, CA

SERVES 10

Who says waffles are just for breakfast? Judy Vandoorne says otherwise, and she should know. She is serious about her waffles. So serious, in fact, that she traveled to Belgium just to learn how to make a truly authentic Belgian waffle. When she returned to the States, she added to her extensive knowledge by dabbling in lesser-known waffle mixes, such as cornmeal. In this dish, she tops a corn bread waffle with a beef and bacon chili for a hearty meal you'll find yourself craving any time of the day.

CORN BREAD WAFFLES

2 cups (473ml) water

2 cups (473ml) milk

½ lb (227g) high-gluten flour

½ lb (227g) fine cornmeal

2 tbsp (19g) instant yeast

5 ½ oz (156g) salted butter, melted

4 oz (113g) lard, melted

1 tbsp (8g) powdered sugar

2 large eggs, separated

BEEF AND BACON CHILI

10 slices thick-cut bacon, chopped

1 ½ large white onions, chopped

1 ½ cloves garlic, minced

2 ½ lb (1134g) ground beef

2 tbsp (14g) chili powder

2 ½ tsp (6g) cumin

2 ½ tsp (6g) smoked paprika

1 tbsp (7g) cayenne pepper

2 ½ tsp (13g) kosher salt

1 ½ (14-oz [392g]) cans whole tomatoes

1 (12-oz [340g]) can tomato sauce

1 (12-oz [352ml]) bottle Mexican beer

2 tsp (10ml) Worcestershire sauce

1 ½ (14-oz [392g]) cans chili beans

Sour cream, for garnish

Cheddar cheese, for garnish

Chopped scallions, for garnish

To make the waffles, in a large bowl, mix the water and the milk together with the high-gluten flour, cornmeal and yeast. Whisk well to get all the dry ingredients incorporated. Add the melted butter, lard and powdered sugar and stir to combine.

Place the egg whites in a separate mixing bowl. Add the egg yolks to the batter and whisk until the egg yolks become incorporated.

Beat the egg whites until medium-stiff peaks form. Fold the egg whites into the batter using a whisk. Let it rise at room temperature, punch down, let it rise again and punch down. Refrigerate overnight.

Add the batter to a waffle maker and cook according to the manufacturer's directions until golden and crispy.

To make the chili, in a skillet over medium heat, cook the bacon until crispy and then pour off most of the bacon fat, reserving 2 tablespoons (30ml). Set the bacon aside. Cook the onion in the bacon fat until translucent, 5 to 6 minutes. Add the minced garlic and cook for an additional minute. Add the beef, breaking up any large clumps, and cook for 5 to 10 minutes, until it is no longer pink.

Put the beef and onion mixture in a large stockpot, add the bacon and dry spices and stir thoroughly. Add the tomatoes, tomato sauce, beer and Worcestershire sauce and stir. Bring to a boil over high heat and boil for 5 minutes, then reduce the heat to medium-low and let it simmer for 2 hours. A half hour before serving, stir in the beans.

Serve the chili in a bowl topped with the sour cream, Cheddar cheese and scallions. Enjoy with the corn bread waffles. (Don't be shy about dipping them in the chili.)

VEGETARIAN POSOLE

GUAC N ROLL—BENJAMIN MILLER—AUSTIN, TX

SERVES 8 TO 10

Benjamin Miller has had a refined palate for as long as he can remember. As a child of five or six, he would demand his mother call ahead to any birthday parties to which he was invited. If the menu didn't meet his approval, no deal. Now, as a grown-up vegetarian he knows what it's like to have your only options be a garden burger or grilled vegetables when eating out. "When people think of vegetarian food," he says, "they think of fake, mock meat." To address this imbalance, Benjamin came up with what he likes to call his "31-Flavor Posole," a composed, elaborate stew hearty and flavorful enough to please carnivores and vegetarians alike. No Tofurkey in sight.

SPICE MIXTURE

2 tsp (5g) paprika

1 tsp cayenne pepper

½ tsp oregano

2 bay leaves

1 tbsp (7g) garlic powder

1 tbsp (7g) onion powder

1 tbsp (7g) cumin

Pinch of black pepper

Pinch of ground cloves

Pinch of cinnamon

Salt to taste

POSOLE

8 tomatillos

2 ears corn, shucked

1 tbsp (15ml) olive oil

2 tbsp (30g) butter

6 red potatoes, peeled and diced

6 carrots, peeled and diced

4 Anaheim peppers, seeded and diced

1 large jalapeño or 2 serrano peppers, seeded and diced

3 poblano peppers (also called pasillas), seeded and diced

4 small red peppers, seeded and diced

4 dried New Mexico or ancho chiles, to float in broth

4 cloves garlic, diced

1 medium white onion, diced

3 large shallots, sliced in half

Handful of cilantro, diced

Water

1 (32-oz [896g]) can hominy, drained

2 handfuls kale, chopped

1 avocado, sliced (optional)

Radish, sliced, for garnish

Queso fresca, for garnish

To make the spice mixture, combine all the ingredients in a bowl.

To make the posole, preheat the broiler. Peel and core the tomatillos. Place the tomatillos, top facing down, along with the corn on a baking sheet and broil until they are brown and black on top. Flip the corn and brown the other side, but not the tomatillos. Cut the kernels off the cob into a bowl. Dice the tomatillos and place in another bowl.

Heat the olive oil and butter in a large pot over medium-low heat. Add the potatoes, carrots, Anaheim peppers, jalapeño, poblanos, red peppers, New Mexico chiles, garlic, onion and shallots to the pot. Bring to a simmer over medium-high heat.

Add the diced tomatillos, cilantro and the spice mixture to the pot. Turn the heat up to high and stir the ingredients for about 5 minutes. Add water to barely cover the ingredients and bring to a simmer, but do not bring to a boil. Lower the heat to medium-low, stirring occasionally for about 20 minutes.

While the potatoes are still firm, add the hominy, kale and roasted corn kernels. Cook for no more than 5 minutes to keep all the vegetables firm.

Garnish each serving with the sliced avocado, sliced radish and queso fresca!

CHAPTER 4

NO MEAT, NO PROBLEM: VEGETARIAN

I've always been an unapologetic, voracious meat eater. All-you-can-eat Korean barbecue joints would fear me. But recently, I tried to eat vegetarian for a month. At first I cursed the world and thought there was no way I would make it a day. It was painful at first. I always felt that meat made dishes taste better. I frequently wolf down all my sides and accoutrements just so I can savor the meat in my dish. But it was talking to my vegetarian friend, Spencer Foxworth, that got me over the hump.

I kept prodding him about how he could really call himself a food lover without being able to eat everything. Spencer told me I had it all wrong. "You become an even bigger lover of food when you can't eat everything," he said. Suddenly, burgers I ate became not about the meat, but about those toppings that I had often overlooked: crisp lettuce, sweet tomatoes and perfectly grilled onions. Chefs put a lot of their soul into crafting all the components in a dish. I finally opened my eyes to them when I couldn't eat everything. These recipes, like Guac N Roll's vegan Guac the Casbah and Tokyo Doggie Style's 100% Homie Veggie Dog are not just for vegetarians or vegans—they're for all the food lovers out there.

THE CINNAMON SNAIL—ADAM SOBEL
NEW YORK, NEW YORK

"You make me want to be a better man." Jack Nicholson laid down this pickup line on Helen Hunt in *As Good as It Gets*, and the collective nation swooned. It has since taken its place as one of the most romantic lines in cinematic history. We don't know whether Chef Adam Sobel has watched this particular scene. But he's certainly lived it.

The story behind Cinnamon Snail begins the way most great stories do. A boy meets a girl. In this case, it was an "adorable vegan girl I fell in love with in Jersey," recalls Adam. "She had a really crappy diet of French fries and canned soup. I wanted to learn how to prepare yummy food for her." And so Adam started his culinary career, cooking and prepping for several vegetarian restaurants until he gained both experience in the food industry and a healthy respect for his girlfriend's ethical and spiritual choices behind her meat- and animal by-product–free diet.

The success and loyal following of a farmers' market–based food stand encouraged him to start a food truck. "We found a really abused-looking old truck on craigslist and, with a few friends of ours, we gutted it and transformed it into what it is today," he says. "You can't even tell it's the same truck." The Cinnamon Snail hit the streets on, appropriately enough, Valentine's Day of 2010 and has been thriving ever since.

Adam's primary goal is to introduce those who may not yet be vegetarian or vegan to inventive, flavorful and nourishing food. "The vegetarian offerings out there tend to lean either toward really bland and wholesome on one end of the spectrum to really processed junk food almost completely devoid of any life and love on the other end of the spectrum," says Adam. " I never really wanted to eat anything like that. I wanted to make food that was exciting and enjoyable, really blow customers' minds and have them leave feeling good."

By the way, he ended up marrying the girl.

LEMONGRASS FIVE-SPICE SEITAN SANDWICH (VEGAN)

THE CINNAMON SNAIL—ADAM SOBEL—NEW YORK, NY

MAKES 3 SANDWICHES

According to Adam Sobel, his Lemongrass Five-Spice Seitan Sandwich "draws inspiration from all over Asia. There are Thai influences from the curried cashews and the lemongrass marinade, a hint of Japan in the wasabi mayo and seitan, and the Szechuan chili sauce and five-spice powder are flavors of China. Served on a crisp French baguette, it's reminiscent of banh mi sandwiches of Vietnam." Adam claims that one ill-conceived attempt to take it off the menu nearly caused riots. "People wanted their Lemongrass Five-Spice Seitan back."

CURRIED CASHEWS

4 cups (643g) raw cashews
¼ cup (59ml) umeboshi plum vinegar
2 ripe medium tomatoes, quartered
1 small red onion, quartered
½ bunch cilantro (leaves and stems)
1 jalapeño chile, stemmed
1" (2.5cm) piece fresh ginger
3 tbsp (45ml) extra-virgin olive oil
2 tbsp (14g) sambar masala
1 tsp asafetida
4 tsp (20g) Thai red curry paste

LEMONGRASS FIVE-SPICE MARINADE

¼ cup (59ml) olive oil
2 stalks lemongrass, cleaned and roughly chopped
2 tbsp (29g) minced fresh ginger
½ cup (20g) chopped cilantro (leaves and stems)
2 tbsp (30g) Thai red curry paste
2 tbsp (14g) five-spice powder
¼ cup (59ml) umeboshi plum vinegar
1 ½ cups (355ml) water

SZECHUAN CHILI SAUCE

⅓ cup (72ml) toasted sesame oil
3 tbsp (22g) red pepper flakes
2 tbsp (15g) black mustard seeds
1 tbsp (7g) chipotle powder
½ tsp ground cloves
½ tsp ground dried ginger
3 tbsp (45ml) agave nectar
⅔ cup (147g) tomato paste
1 cup (236ml) water

WASABI MAYONNAISE

1 ¾ cups (385g) vegan mayonnaise (we like Vegenaise)
¼ cup (29g) natural wasabi powder (we prefer Eden brand or Sushi Sonic)
¼ cup (59ml) mirin
1 tbsp (15ml) nama shoyu (unpasteurized soy sauce)
1 tbsp (22g) brown rice syrup

SANDWICHES

3 tbsp (45ml) olive oil
3 ¾ cups (568g) chopped seitan
1 wide French baguette
3 cups (120g) arugula

(continued)

LEMONGRASS FIVE-SPICE SEITAN SANDWICH (VEGAN)

To make the cashews, place the cashews in a medium bowl. Put the plum vinegar, tomatoes, onion, cilantro, jalapeño, ginger, olive oil, sambar masala, asafetida and curry paste in a blender. Blend at high speed for 30 seconds. Pour the puree over the cashews. Mix briefly to distribute evenly. Allow the mixture to rest for 30 minutes.

Carefully spread the cashews and all the liquid on a single dehydrator tray with a teflex sheet. Dehydrate at 112°F (44°C) for 24 hours. Remove the teflex sheet, placing the cashews directly on the dehydrator screen. Continue to dehydrate for 24 more hours. These cashews can stay fresh for 2 months if stored in an airtight container.

To make the marinade, heat the olive oil in a small saucepan over a medium heat. Add the lemongrass and ginger, and sauté for 2 to 3 minutes, stirring until the ginger becomes fragrant and golden. Add the remaining ingredients and bring to a boil over medium-high heat. Cover the pot and turn off the heat. Allow the ingredients to steep and soften in the hot water for 15 minutes.

Pour the contents of the pot into a blender and blend at high speed for 45 seconds to form a smooth marinade. Chill the marinade until ready to use. The marinade will keep for up to 8 days in the refrigerator, and it also works well as a marinade for vegetables and tofu.

To make the chili sauce, heat the sesame oil in a small saucepan over medium heat. When the oil is hot, add the red pepper flakes, mustard seeds, chipotle powder, cloves and dried ginger and stir for 40 to 60 seconds until fragrant but not too dark. Place the fried spices and oil into a blender along with the agave nectar, tomato paste and water. Blend on high speed for 45 seconds to form a smooth, emulsified sauce.

To make the wasabi mayo, mix all the ingredients rapidly with a whisk until the mixture is smooth and free of lumps. This mayonnaise will stay fresh for up to 3 weeks when stored in an airtight container in the refrigerator and is great on many types of sandwiches.

To assemble the sandwiches, heat the olive oil in a pan or cast-iron skillet over medium heat. When the oil is hot, add the chopped seitan and sauté for 4 to 6 minutes, until the seitan is seared and golden brown in spots. Pour ¾ cup (180ml) of the marinade onto the seitan and allow it to cook and soak in the marinade for another 2 minutes.

Cut the baguette into three 8- to 10-inch (20 to 25cm) portions and slice open. Toast the baguettes in a pan, cut-side down. Spread 2 to 3 tablespoons (30 to 45g) of wasabi mayo on each half of the baguette. Place 1 cup (40g) of the arugula on each bottom half of the baguette, followed by 1 ¼ cups (190g) of the cooked seitan, followed by 2 tablespoons (30ml) of the Szechuan chili sauce. Sprinkle each sandwich with ¼ to ⅓ cup (40 to 50g) of the curried cashews and cover with the top half of the baguette.

BOURBON PECAN PANCAKES WITH GINGER STOUT SYRUP (VEGAN)

THE CINNAMON SNAIL—ADAM SOBEL—NEW YORK, NY

MAKES 8 TO 10 PANCAKES

To Adam Sobel, these Bourbon Pecan Pancakes are what The Cinnamon Snail is all about. Pecans freshly roasted with bourbon and spices take boring ol' pancakes and turn them on their head. Adam believes they're good enough to make even the staunchest meat eater think twice. "What about your dad? He thinks your vegan diet is weird, right? Why don't you make him eat the best damn pancakes he ever ate in his life? Make everyone you know who doesn't get veganism some SERIOUSLY BOMB, absurdly good pancakes."

Note: You will want to make the cardamom butter in advance, so it can set up nicely in the refrigerator. Plan to make it the day before, so you can get a nice, pretty butter pat out of it on your hot steaming pancakes.

CARDAMOM BUTTER
½ cup (122ml) soy milk
2 tbsp (30ml) rice vinegar
2 tbsp (44ml) maple syrup
½ tsp salt
1 tsp ground cardamom
¼ tsp ground cloves
1 cup (235ml) refined coconut oil, melted
3 tbsp (45ml) extra-virgin olive oil
2 tbsp (11g) soy lecithin granules
½ tsp xanthan gum

GINGER STOUT SYRUP
2 tbsp (15g) ground dried ginger
1 tsp (3g) cinnamon
½ tsp black pepper
1 (12-oz [340ml]) bottle stout beer
2 cups (473ml) maple syrup

BOURBON CANDIED PECANS
2 cups (241g) pecan pieces
½ cup (118ml) evaporated cane juice
¼ cup (59ml) bourbon
½ tsp salt
1 tsp cinnamon
2 tbsp (30ml) canola oil

PANCAKE BATTER
1 ½ cups (149g) all-purpose flour
2 tsp (7g) baking powder
2 tsp (9g) baking soda
½ tsp salt
¼ cup (88ml) maple syrup
1 ⅔ cups (394ml) soy milk
3 tbsp (45ml) canola oil
1 tsp vanilla extract

Vegan butter or canola oil, for greasing the griddle
Dash of cinnamon or powdered sugar (optional)

(continued)

BOURBON PECAN PANCAKES WITH GINGER STOUT SYRUP (VEGAN)

To make the cardamom butter, place the soy milk, rice vinegar, maple syrup, salt, cardamom and cloves in a blender and mix on high speed for 10 seconds. After a minute or so, the soy milk will have curdled to a thick consistency like buttermilk. Add the melted coconut oil, olive oil, lecithin and xanthan gum. Blend on high speed for 60 seconds to thoroughly emulsify.

Pour into a pint container (or if you wish to cut it into sticks, into a 4 x 4-inch [10 x 10cm] container), and chill in the freezer for an hour. Transfer the tub to the refrigerator and use as needed, or slice and wrap with parchment paper into even ½-cup (114g) sticks.

To make the syrup, place the ginger, cinnamon and black pepper in a large saucepot. Whisking continuously to avoid clumping, slowly pour in the stout beer and maple syrup. Bring to a boil over medium heat. Turn the heat down to low, and simmer for 30 minutes uncovered. Chill in a bottle or an airtight container and use within 3 weeks.

To make the candied pecans, preheat the oven to 350°F (180°C, or gas mark 4). Mix all the ingredients together and distribute evenly on a parchment-covered sheet pan. Bake for 12 minutes, flipping the pecans halfway through to ensure even baking. Allow the pecans to cool and break up any large clusters. Store at room temperature.

To make the batter, whisk together the flour, baking powder, baking soda and salt in a mixing bowl. Make a well in the center of the dry ingredients, and add the maple syrup, soy milk, canola oil and vanilla extract. Whisk together to form a smooth batter.

Heat a skillet or griddle over medium heat. Lightly oil the pan with vegan butter. Ladle the pancake batter evenly, forming pancakes in any size you like. Sprinkle onto each circle of batter 2 to 3 tablespoons (15 to 23g) of bourbon pecans. Carefully flip the pancakes when bubbles start to appear close to the center and the edges start to brown lightly and lift away from the pan. Cook on the other side for the same amount of time.

Plate 3 or 4 pancakes per serving, top with a pat of the cardamom butter, a generous drizzle of the stout syrup, a sprinkle of bourbon pecans and a dash of cinnamon or powdered sugar.

FALAFEL MEZZE PLATE

CHICKPEADX—YAIR MAIDAN—PORTLAND, OR

MAKES 20 FALAFEL

Yair Maidan boasts a good fifteen years of cooking experience, some spent in Michelin-starred restaurants. Yet neither his resume nor his culinary education at Ferrandi in France was getting him the restaurant positions he desired. So he decided to create his own opportunities by starting up a food cart. He discovered Washington State grows 95 percent of the chickpeas consumed in the U.S., yet the regional cuisine wasn't taking full advantage of this local, affordable crop. And what better way to feature a chickpea than by grinding it, seasoning it and frying it up to crisp, golden perfection?

SUPER TAHINI SAUCE

2 cloves garlic, thinly sliced
2 tsp (10g) Sriracha sauce
1 tsp simple syrup or honey
Juice of 1 lemon
Juice of 1 lime
Salt to taste
8 oz (227g) tahini paste
1 cup (237ml) cold water
salt to taste

ZHUG (HOT SAUCE)

1 ½ tbsp (11g) cumin
¾ tbsp (5g) coriander
1 ½ tbsp (23g) black pepper
1 tsp cardamom seeds
¼ ounce (7g) dried Thai chile
1 ½ oz (42g) fresh serrano chile
¼ ounce (7g) fresh Thai chile
2 oz (57g) garlic
1 tbsp (15g) citric acid
Salt to taste
4 ½ oz (128g) Italian flat-leaf parsley
6 oz (170g) cilantro

FALAFEL

1 ¼ lb (567g) dried whole chickpeas
1 cup (235ml) cold water
2 tsp (9g) baking soda
1 lb (454g) yellow onion
1 ¾ oz (50g) garlic
5 oz (142g) Italian parsley (about 1 bunch)
2 ½ oz (71g) cilantro (about 1 bunch)
1 ½ oz (43g) serrano chiles
1 tbsp (8g) whole coriander
1 ½ tsp (8g) black pepper
1 tbsp (8g) whole cumin
1 tbsp (15g) mild curry powder
1 ½ tsp (8g) red pepper flakes
3 tsp (15g) kosher salt
1 tsp baking powder
Rice bran oil
½ cup (50g) chickpea flour

To make the tahini sauce, place the garlic, Sriracha, simple syrup or honey, lemon and lime juices, and a pinch of salt in a blender and puree on high speed until everything is well blended and smooth. Transfer the mixture to a stand mixer. Add the tahini paste and whisk using the whisk attachment. Slowly add some of the cold water to achieve the desired consistency. The tahini paste is strange in how it accepts liquid. It will get thicker at first, and then turn into a smooth, velvety sauce. Also, the mixture should be slightly thinner than you would think because it will thicken up after it sits for some time. Add salt to taste.

To make the zhug, put the cumin, coriander, black pepper and cardamom seeds in a skillet over medium heat and toast to maximize flavor. Just before the spices are ready (when you can start to smell them), add the dried chiles. Put this aside for about 10 minutes; the spices will grind better if they are not too hot.

Slice the fresh chiles and garlic. Place in a blender with the citric acid, a pinch of salt and the ground spices. Add just enough water to cover and puree on high speed until you have a smooth paste.

Roughly chop the herbs. If the stems are not too woody, feel free to include them. The cilantro stems in particular have a good flavor and tend to be soft. Add to the blender along with a bit more water and puree until you achieve a sauce-like consistency. The last and most important step is to taste the zhug and salt to taste.

To make the falafel, soak the chickpeas in a large container covered by at least 4 inches (10cm) of cold water with 1 teaspoon of the baking soda overnight.

Roughly chop the onions, garlic, parsley, cilantro and serranos. Toast the coriander, black pepper and cumin in a skillet over medium heat until they are 90 percent done (when the coriander begins to pop). Add the curry powder and red pepper flakes, toast a little more, then let cool. Grind the mix in a spice mill. Drain and rinse the chickpeas. Combine with the spice mix, kosher salt and chopped vegetables. Grind in a meat grinder.

Place the uncovered falafel mixture in the refrigerator to relax for at least 1 hour. Combine the remaining 1 teaspoon baking soda, baking powder and cold water. Add to the falafel mix. Form the falafel balls using 2 spoons or a small ice cream scoop. You can also hand roll them like a meatball.

Pour the oil into a deep pot or fryer to a depth of 4 to 5 inches (10 to 15cm) and heat to 350°F (177°C). Fry a ball of falafel. If it falls apart, add the chickpea flour to the mix. Fry the falafel in batches, being careful not to crowd the pot, bringing the oil back to temperature between batches. Let drain on paper towels and salt to taste.

Serve the falafel with the tahini sauce and the zhug on the side.

GUAC THE CASBAH

GUAC N ROLL—BENJAMIN MILLER—AUSTIN, TX

SERVES 1

Benjamin Miller is rethinking his habit of recommending any other of his guacamoles but this one to newcomers. "When people come up to the truck, I tend to refer them to a basic, traditional guacamole," he says. "But then when people venture out and ignore me, they get the Casbah and go crazy over it." Ben is constantly challenging the misperception that guacamole can't be a meal on its own. He mashes his avocados to order and tops them with enough filling ingredients to leave the hungriest person satisfied. In this dish, the rich, full flavors of hummus and avocado are brightened and highlighted by fresh mint and cucumber. He swears he came up with the name, Guac the Casbah. His wife Ashlea begs to differ. Either way, this isn't your average guacamole. You will have plenty of hummus left over. Store in an airtight container in the refrigerator for up to a week.

HUMMUS

1 (15-oz [425g]) can chickpeas, drained

1 tbsp (9g) diced white onion

2 tbsp (5g) chopped fresh Italian parsley

1 tbsp (15ml) olive oil, or more as needed

Juice of ½ lime

Salt to taste

CASBAH CUCUMBER SALAD

¼ medium cucumber, diced

1 tsp toasted sesame seeds

1 tbsp (9g) raisins

1 tsp chopped fresh mint

Salt to taste

Drizzle of olive oil

1 avocado, peeled and seeded

Juice of ½ lime, or to taste

Salt to taste

Sprinkle of cumin

Sprinkle of cayenne

To make the hummus, add the chickpeas, white onion, Italian parsley, olive oil and lime juice to a blender and puree until smooth. Add salt to taste.

To make the cucumber salad, combine the cucumber, sesame seeds, raisins and mint in a small bowl. Lightly salt and mix with a few drops of olive oil.

In a separate bowl, mash the avocado with 1 ½ tablespoons (23g) of hummus, lime juice, salt, cumin and cayenne. Place the avocado mixture in a bowl for serving. Top with the cucumber salad. Serve with warm tortilla chips.

100% HOMIE VEGGIE DOG

TOKYO DOGGIE STYLE—CHEF KEITH YOKOYAMA AND ALLIE YAMAMOTO—LOS ANGELES, CA

MAKES 8 TO 10 HOT DOGS

Allie Yamamoto explains that the gourmet, Japanese-inspired hot dogs she serves are a direct reflection of her and Chef Keith Yokoyama. She was born and raised in Japan, while Keith is a native Southern Californian. "We merged our knowledge and passion and came up with Japanese fusion comfort food." Asian-inspired hot dogs are quickly becoming all the rage, but that doesn't mean vegetarians have to feel left out. These made-from-scratch veggie dogs have wasabi mayo and pickled daikon for an exciting bite.

YUZU MAYO DRESSING

1 cup (220g) Kewpie mayonnaise

4 tbsp (59ml) freshly squeezed yuzu juice (if not, bottled yuzu juice)

3 tbsp (44ml) mirin

1 tsp sesame oil

3 tbsp (44ml) canola oil

YUZU CITRUS ASIAN SLAW

1 cup (340g) shredded green cabbage

½ cup (170g) julienned carrot

½ cup (65g) thinly sliced onion

¼ cup (85g) chopped kimchi

2 tbsp (5g) whole-leaf cilantro

VEGGIE DOGS

¼ cup (12g) prepared hijiki

¼ cup (50g) shelled edamame

¼ cup (38g) chopped onion

¼ cup (85g) shredded cabbage

1 tbsp (14g) minced ginger

1 tbsp (10g) minced garlic

2 tbsp (5g) chopped cilantro

1 cup (161g) cooked brown rice

10 cooked red potatoes

Canola oil, for grilling

Kosher salt

8 to 10 New England–style hot dog buns

½ cup (112g) salted butter

¼ cup (48g) sugar

Wasabi mayonnaise, for serving

Teriyaki sauce, for serving

Aonori flakes (seaweed flakes), for serving

Fukujinzuke pickled daikon, chopped, for serving

Whole-leaf cilantro, for garnish

To make the yuzu mayo dressing, combine the Kewpie mayonnaise, yuzu juice, mirin, sesame oil and canola oil in a small bowl and mix thoroughly until well blended.

For the yuzu citrus Asian slaw, combine the green cabbage, carrot, onion, kimchi and cilantro in a bowl. Add the yuzu mayo dressing and toss to coat.

To make the veggie dogs, in a bowl, mix the hijiki, edamame, onion, cabbage, ginger, garlic, cilantro and brown rice thoroughly. Dice the cooked red potato and mix it in batches until the mixture binds to form patties. Take 1.7 ounces (48g) of the mix and shape into a 1 x 6-inch (2.5 x 15cm) patty.

Oil a grill pan, add the patty and a sprinkling of salt, and cook over medium heat for 2 to 3 minutes, until crispy on the outside. Flip and cook the other side.

While cooking the patty, prepare the hot dog buns. Mix the salted butter with a small amount of sugar and spread it on the outside of the bun. Toast both sides for 30 seconds, or until golden brown. When the patty is done, place it in the bun and top it with the Asian slaw. Drizzle wasabi mayonnaise and teriyaki sauce on top, and garnish with the aonori flakes, chopped fukujinzuke pickled daikon and whole-leaf cilantro.

BLACK BEAN AND CORN BALLS

BARONE MEATBALL COMPANY—STEPHEN DEWEY—RALEIGH/DURHAM, NC

MAKES ABOUT 15 MEATBALLS

In the process of following his dream of owning an Italian restaurant, Stephen Dewey hit upon a startling truth. "I realized I could pretty much make any recipe into a meatball. You take out a little bit of this, add a little bit of that, and bam, you have a meatball." And Barone Meatball Company was born. Of course, the "meat" part of meatball is entirely optional. Inspired by his vegetarian wife, these Black Bean and Corn Balls have cumin, chili powder and jalapeño for a distinctly Southwestern feel. Perfect for serving up on a pita.

2 (15-oz [420g]) cans black beans
½ cup (75g) corn kernels
1 egg
1 cup (121g) bread crumbs
1 ½ tsp (4g) cumin
1 tbsp (7g) chili powder
3 cloves garlic, chopped
1 jalapeño, chopped
½ onion, chopped
Salt and pepper to taste
Cooking spray

Preheat the oven to 400°F (200°C, or gas mark 6). Drain the liquid from the cans of black beans. Mash up the black beans and mix in the corn, egg, bread crumbs, cumin, chili powder, garlic, jalapeño, onion and salt and pepper. Mix well.

Coat a cookie sheet with cooking spray. Roll the mixture into 1-inch (2.5cm) diameter balls and place on the cookie sheet. Coat the tops of the balls with cooking spray.

Bake in the oven for 20 minutes, flipping the balls halfway through. The balls will get a little darker and become crispy on the outside.

SANTA FE BLACK BEAN BURGER

MIX'D UP FOOD TRUCK—BRETT EANES—ATLANTA, GA

MAKES 8 BURGERS

There are those who grow up knowing exactly what they want to do in life, as certain as they know their own name. Brett Eanes is one of those people. "I grew up around restaurants. I started in the food industry when I was 15 and just didn't stop. The passion for food and the desire to create something that has a wow factor just kept growing." His favorite vehicle for delivering that wow factor is a good burger. "If I can trick them out and blow you away, I've succeeded." This black bean burger with pico de gallo, avocado puree, ancho mayo and cheese is sure to do just that.

PICO DE GALLO
2 Roma tomatoes, diced
¼ onion, diced
½ lime, juiced
4–5 cilantro stems and leaves, chopped
Salt and black pepper to taste

ANCHO MAYONNAISE
1 cup (220g) mayonnaise
1 tbsp (7g) ancho chile powder
1 tsp chili powder
1 tsp paprika
1 tsp black pepper

AVOCADO PUREE
2 ripened avocados
Juice of 1 lime
Pinch of salt
Pinch of cilantro

BLACK BEAN PATTIES
¼ cup (60ml) canola oil
22 oz (624g) corn
½ onion, diced
2 cloves garlic, minced
2 oz (57g) roasted red peppers, diced
Pinch of dried thyme
Pinch of red pepper flakes
3 lb (1361g) cooked black beans
1 tsp black pepper
½ tsp ground coriander
1 ½ tsp (4g) ground cumin
1 ½ tsp (4g) chili powder
1 tsp garlic powder
1 tsp paprika
3 ½ oz (99g) Rice Chex, processed to panko consistency
1 egg
1 tsp kosher salt

8 burger buns

To make the pico de gallo, combine the tomatoes, onions, lime juice, cilantro and salt and pepper in a bowl. Set aside.

To make the ancho mayonnaise, combine the mayonnaise, ancho chili powder, chili powder, paprika and black pepper in a bowl. Set aside.

To make the avocado puree, combine the ingredients in a blender and puree, or mix by hand.

To make the patties, coat a sauté pan with oil and heat until shimmering. Add the corn and sauté over high heat for 2 minutes. Add the onion, garlic, peppers, thyme and red pepper flakes, and sauté for another 3 minutes. Transfer to a sheet pan to cool evenly.

In a mixer with the paddle attachment, beat three-fourths of the black beans to a somewhat smooth consistency. Add the cooled corn mixture, slowly mixing until incorporated. Add the pepper, coriander, cumin, chili powder, garlic powder, paprika and salt and mix thoroughly. Mix in the Rice Chex until incorporated, then the egg. Blend in the remaining one-fourth whole black beans.

Preheat the oven to 400°F (200°C, or gas mark 6). On a lined sheet pan, form the patties about 1 inch (2.5cm) thick. Bake for 18 minutes and let cool in the refrigerator for at least 4 hours.

When time to serve, heat the oil in a pan and fry the patty for 4 to 5 minutes, until crisp on both sides. Place on the burger bun and top with the pico de gallo, avocado puree and ancho mayonnaise.

BE LOVIN' VEGGIES

MELTS MY HEART—WES ISIP—SAN JOSE, CA

MAKES 1 SANDWICH

A visit to a popular grilled cheese truck in Southern California and a little market research convinced owner Brian Aflague that his love for grilled cheese was a universal love. "It's such an easy concept: bread, butter and cheese," Brian explains. "But what's great about it is it has so much stretch, so much range and versatility. There's so much you can do with it." Brian displays this versatility at his Melts My Heart truck with sandwiches like the Be Lovin' Veggies, a gorgeous blend of veggies and cheese kicked up with Sriracha. With the limited refrigeration space on a food truck, Brian goes through his ingredients pretty quickly. He shops every other day to ensure his veggies are as fresh as possible. Trust us, you'll taste the difference it makes.

1 tbsp (14ml) olive oil

3 cremini mushrooms, sliced

¼ yellow onion, chopped

¼ red onion, chopped

¼ tsp minced garlic

½ scallion, chopped

Salt and pepper

Butter

2 slices sourdough bread

2 ½ slices mild Cheddar cheese

1 ½ tsp (7ml) Sriracha sauce

2 slices tomato

3 small leaves fresh basil

1 small avocado, peeled, pitted, and sliced

Heat the olive oil in a large pan over medium-high heat. Add the cremini mushrooms and yellow and red onions to the pan. Sauté for about 4 minutes, stirring frequently.

Reduce the heat to low, add the minced garlic and continue to sauté for about 2 minutes. Stir continuously to avoid burning.

Add the scallion and a pinch each of salt and pepper and stir for 1 minute. The sautéed ingredients should be tender and a little crunchy with a light brown color. Transfer to a bowl and set aside.

Raise the heat to medium-high. Butter one side of each slice of sourdough bread and set the buttered-sides down onto the pan. Spread the cheese over both slices of bread. In a zigzag motion from one side of the bread to the other, squeeze on the Sriracha sauce. Add more to taste for increased flavor and spiciness.

Add the sautéed vegetables, tomatoes, fresh basil and avocado on top of the cheese on one slice of bread. Add the other slice of bread on top of the ingredients, buttered-side up. Toast both sides of the sandwich for 2 to 3 minutes, until crispy and golden brown.

SWEET POTATO GRITS WITH VEGETABLE RAGÙ AND RED PEPPER ROMESCO

DELI-ICIOUS—SUSAN TOWER AND TY PARKER—RALEIGH, NC

SERVES 6 TO 8

Susan Tower, a former audio engineer, was working in the restaurant industry when she started to feel the tug of the road. Using her old connections in the music scene, she started touring with bands again until one fateful snowstorm delayed her flight in Chicago. A conversation with a stranger resulted in her moving to North Carolina, where she now runs a health-focused food truck. "I don't want people to walk away feeling empty or feeling full of saturated fats," says Susan of her fresh, seasonal, often local food. "I want to make sure that I can feel good about what I put out there, and it's a healthy, balanced and flavorful meal." There's certainly nothing to feel bad about in these sweet potato grits with vegetable ragù. Hearty vegetable and creamy sweet potatoes practically sing with a red pepper romesco.

SWEET POTATO GRITS

2 large sweet potatoes

2 cups (473ml) whole milk

2 cups (473ml) water

2 cups (421g) grits

1 cup (121g) shredded Cheddar cheese

4 oz (113g) shredded Gouda cheese

2 oz (57g) cream cheese

Salt to taste

VEGETABLE RAGÙ

2 tbsp (28ml) olive oil

1 eggplant, diced into ½" (1.3cm) pieces

1 red bell pepper, cored, seeded and julienned

1 green (or yellow) squash, diced into ½" (1.3cm) pieces

1 large yellow onion, julienned

RED PEPPER ROMESCO

4 oz (112g) French bread or any crusty bread

2 oz (57g) toasted almonds

8 oz (226g) roasted red peppers or 1 red bell pepper, cored and sautéed until soft

½ cup (118ml) olive oil

1 clove garlic, minced

Salt to taste

Preheat the oven to 350°F (180°C, or gas mark 4).

To make the grits, peel and halve the sweet potatoes. Bake for 25 to 30 minutes until the potatoes are soft. Add the potatoes to a blender and puree until smooth; set aside. Keep the oven on.

Bring the milk and water to a boil in a pot over medium-high heat. Reduce the heat to a simmer and slowly pour in the grits while stirring. When the grits thicken in 10 to 15 minutes, add the pureed sweet potatoes, Cheddar cheese, Gouda cheese, cream cheese and salt. Stir until the sweet potatoes become incorporated.

To make the vegetable ragù, add the olive oil to a medium sauté pan over medium heat. Add the eggplant, red bell pepper, squash and onion and sauté for 5 to 7 minutes, until soft.

To make the red pepper romesco, toast the bread in the oven for 8 to 10 minutes, until golden brown. In a food processor or blender, add the almonds, roasted red peppers, olive oil and garlic and puree until smooth. Crumble the bread into the mixture and puree again until smooth. The sauce should be slightly thickened. Add more bread if you desire a thicker sauce. Season with salt to taste.

Spoon the grits into a bowl, add the vegetable ragù and top off with ¼ to ⅓ cup (60 to 80ml) of red pepper romesco.

ROASTED ROOTS SALAD

THE MORAL OMNIVORE—ROSS AND LINNEA LOGAS—MINNEAPOLIS, MN

SERVES 4 TO 6

"There are so many vegetables out there, and so many things you can do with them," said Ross and Linnea Logas. The variety of veggies wasn't the only reason why The Moral Omnivore focuses on produce. Vegetable-heavy cuisine is a more sustainable way of eating so Linnea saw their food truck as a way to have a positive social impact. One fateful meal involving cauliflower and garlic set them on a quest that ultimately taught them that sometimes simple is best. "We went to a restaurant and had roasted cauliflower with roasted garlic. It was an amazing combination, and I knew that I could find something to do with it," recalls Linnea. They tried cauliflower gnocchi, they tried veggie burgers, but nothing was quite right. It wasn't until they were snacking on leftovers of a failed experiment that it struck them. Earthy root veggies, sweet apple and cardamom, and savory garlic make an elegant salad.

---

1 cup (210g) dry red quinoa

3 cups (710ml) water

1 head cauliflower

5 to 6 parsnips

5 cloves garlic, minced

3 tbsp (45ml) olive oil

½ tsp nutmeg

1 tsp coriander

½ tsp cardamom

¼ cup (59ml) lemon juice, divided

Salt and pepper to taste

1 Granny Smith apple, diced

2 carrots, diced

**BROWN BUTTER BALSAMIC
SALAD DRESSING**

6 tbsp (86g) butter

2 tbsp (30ml) balsamic vinegar

Preheat oven to 350°F (177°C).

Put the dry red quinoa in a pot with the water on high heat. When the water starts to simmer after 3 to 4 minutes, turn down the heat to medium. Let the quinoa cook for 10 minutes or until the grains open up into spirals. Do not stir. Let it sit until all the water is absorbed.

Finely dice the cauliflower florets and parsnips. Combine with garlic, olive oil, nutmeg, coriander, cardamom, 2 tablespoons (30ml) of lemon juice and salt and pepper to taste. Place on a lined cookie sheet and bake for 15 to 20 minutes until lightly browned.

While the cauliflower and parsnips are baking, finely dice the apple and soak it in the remaining lemon juice combined with enough water to cover the apple.

To make the salad dressing, heat the butter in a saucepan over medium heat stirring constantly. When the foam begins to lessen and the butter turns a golden brown, about 3 minutes, turn off the heat. Let the butter cool for at least 1 minute and stir in the balsamic vinegar. Let the dressing cool.

After baking, allow the salad to cool for about 7 minutes. Strain the apples and toss the salad with apples, diced carrots and salad dressing to taste.

CHAPTER 5

FOOD WITH FLAIR: LATIN AMERICAN

In my early twenties, I had a great job as a manager and was moving up in the company but made the impulsive decision to move to Mexico and do humanitarian work. I was chastised by many, and somewhere along the way even convinced myself it was a foolish mistake. But looking back, it was one of the best experiences of my life.

What I loved most about Mexico was the culture around food. People in my small town of Jerez, Zacatecas, started hearing about my love for food, and I was often invited to people's homes for dinner. Because I spoke zero Spanish when I arrived, the conversations were light but I always ate everything in front of me. These home chefs were communicating who they were to me through food and by eating and loving the food they spent all day cooking for me, I was communicating my acceptance and respect.

There's more to Latin American food than Mexican food. The mobile food revolution has done an amazing job of introducing new cultural foods to the masses. Chefs and owners passionate about their countries' foods now have an outlet to express themselves. Take La Cocinita in New Orleans. They are introducing countless people every day to Venezuelan food like their arepas filled with brisket. Or take El Fuego in D.C., proudly showcasing Peruvian dishes like Lomo Saltado. These food cart owners are communicating their cultures to people every day with every dish they serve. It's easy for us to show our appreciation for putting themselves out there. Just enjoy their delicious food in this chapter.

EL FUEGO DC—MANUEL ALFARO
WASHINGTON, D.C.

When Puerto Rican-born Manuel Alfaro met his Peruvian wife Maria, he didn't just fall in love with the woman; he also fell in love with her country.

For as long as he can remember, Manuel has always had a strong connection with food. "I've always enjoyed the culinary arts. I was born into them," he explains. "It comes from the family. Since I was a little kid, I was always in the kitchen, following along with my mother." That love of the kitchen would follow Manuel throughout his entire life, spurring him to study the culinary arts in Spain. From there, Manuel's resume is a medley of positions in the food industry, from general manager to chef to seafood exporter. It was at one of these jobs that he met Maria, also a veteran of restaurant operations, and the rest, as they say, is history.

It was the birth of their first child that sparked their visit to Maria's home country of Peru to meet the rest of her family. Manuel hasn't been the same since. "I actually fell in love with not just Peru as a country, but the culture, the people, and, most importantly of all, the food," he recalls. "Since then I've been learning about the many facets of Peruvian cuisine."

Manuel's sole mission since then has been to introduce his newfound passion to the rest of the States. "Being able to diffuse the Peruvian gastronomy to our nation's capital is what really pinpointed the choosing of the concept and cuisine of my food truck, El Fuego." His mission has been a huge success. Manuel's food truck (a converted fire response vehicle complete with emergency lights, fire suppression nozzles and the works) not only serves authentic Peruvian dishes on the streets of D.C. but also, thanks to a connection with the Peruvian embassy, can be spotted at V.I.P functions and has even been awarded the 2013 Innovation in Diffusing Peruvian Cuisine in the U.S. Award by the Peruvian American Chef's Association. "I'm truly Peruvian at heart."

LOMO SALTADO

EL FUEGO DC—MANUEL ALFARO AND OMAR RODRIGUEZ VALLADARES—WASHINGTON, D.C.

SERVES 2

Every Peruvian family has its way of making Lomo Saltado. You may wonder why the national dish of Peru is made with soy sauce and cooked in a wok. "The main thing about Peruvian cuisine is that it's always been about infusion," Manuel Alfaro says. "Throughout the past couple of hundred years, you've had an influx of different cultures, from Japanese, to Chinese, to Italian, even Argentinean, throughout the Southern Hemisphere, and all of these cultures are infused into Peruvian cuisine." One of the key components of Lomo Saltado is the vibrant veggies stir-fried to crisp perfection. This dish pairs well with white rice or French fries.

COOKING SAUCE

⅓ cup (79ml) olive oil

¼ cup (59ml) soy sauce (we prefer wheat-free, naturally brewed)

¼ cup (59ml) rice vinegar

½ tsp sesame oil

2 cloves garlic, minced

1 tbsp (14g) minced ginger

Salt and pepper to taste

½ lb (227g) beef tenderloin, cut into ¼" (6mm)-thick strips (always cut beef against the grain, which ensures tenderness)

1 medium red onion, cut into ½" (1.3cm)-thick strips

2 jalapeño peppers, seeded and deveined (this is a substitution; the dish is traditionally prepared with fresh Peruvian yellow peppers), cut into ¼" (6mm)-thick strips.

2 plum tomatoes, quartered

Small bunch fresh cilantro, finely chopped

To make the cooking sauce, place the olive oil, soy sauce, rice vinegar, sesame oil, garlic and ginger in a blender. Add salt and pepper to taste. Blend until smooth and set aside.

Heat a skillet or wok over high heat until it starts smoking. Add about 1 tablespoon (14ml) of the cooking sauce, and when it starts smoking, add the beef. Sear the meat by stir-frying for 1 to 2 minutes. When the meat is well seared, add the onion, jalapeño and another 1 tablespoon (14ml) of the cooking sauce. Stir-fry for 30 seconds and add the tomatoes, a pinch or two of finely chopped fresh cilantro and 1 tablespoon (14ml) of the cooking sauce. Stir fry-for another 20 seconds, and sprinkle a pinch of cilantro on top.

CEVICHE MIXTO

EL FUEGO DC—MANUEL ALFARO AND OMAR RODRIGUEZ VALLADARES—WASHINGTON, D.C

SERVES 2

"You cannot consider yourself a Peruvian restaurant if you're not serving ceviche," opines Manuel Alfaro. Unfortunately, Manuel doesn't have a restaurant-size kitchen in which to make and serve the giant platters of the seafood dish often seen in most dining establishments. So he scaled it down a bit and offers it as an appetizer. Manuel says he regularly hears his customers sing his ceviche's praises. The acidity of the red onion and citrus elevate the tilapia and shrimp to whole new levels of fresh.

4 oz (112g) medium (51–60 count) raw shrimp

2 stalks celery, diced

¼ cup (59ml) water

2 habañero peppers, diced

1 tsp minced ginger

2 cloves garlic

2 tbsp (30ml) milk

2 (9-oz [255g]) fillets fresh tilapia, into ¼" (6mm) strips

1 small red onion, julienned, plus more for garnish

Juice of 3 large juicy limes

Pinch of fresh cilantro, plus more for garnish

Salt and white pepper to taste

Place the shrimp and 1 stalk of the celery in a small saucepan, add the water and cook over high heat for 3 to 4 minutes, until the shrimp turn pink. Remove from the heat, drain and reserve the liquid, and discard the celery. Rinse the shrimp in cold water to stop the cooking process and set aside. Place the shrimp and cooking liquid in the refrigerator until chilled.

Add 1 of the habañero peppers, ginger, garlic and remaining stalk of celery to a blender along with the cooking liquid from the shrimp and milk. Blend until smooth and strain.

In a 9 x 11-inch (23 x 28cm) plastic pan, place the fish, shrimp, remaining habañero, onion, the blended ingredients, lime juice and a pinch of cilantro. Add salt and pepper to taste and gently mix well. Place in the refrigerator for 10 minutes and then mix again. Keep in the refrigerator for another 10 minutes until ready to serve.

Mix before serving and garnish with the onion and cilantro.

GARLIC CARNE ASADA QUESADILLA

333 TRUCK—ERIC CHUNG—SAN JOSE, CA

MAKES 8 QUESADILLAS

Eric Chung started his culinary school in San Francisco, interning for the Ritz-Carlton hotel. The French-style cuisine wasn't speaking to him, so he jumped at the chance to work the Asian station in the Apple cafeteria. There he met fellow chef Angel Santos and, together with Eric's girlfriend Bonnie Lui, they decided to open up a food truck. "The whole reason why we started the 333 Food Truck was because we felt there was a niche that wasn't filled before we entered it, something between a restaurant and fast food," he says. "Something quick and convenient that doesn't sacrifice health. Something with a price point lower than a sit-down restaurant that you can feel good about eating." His Garlic Carne Asada Quesadilla, with cilantro and jalapeño-glazed sirloin steak and an avocado garlic sauce, nails it.

CARNE ASADA
1 ½ lb (680g) sirloin steak
Salt to taste
Light chili powder to taste
Dark chili powder to taste

CARNE ASADA GLAZE
4 oz (113g) garlic
Juice of 2 limes
½ bunch cilantro
1 jalapeño pepper, seeded
2 ½ tsp (13g) salt
7 ½ tbsp (99ml) oil

AVOCADO GARLIC SAUCE
1 avocado, peeled, pitted, and diced
6 cloves garlic
Juice of 1 ½ limes
1 tsp salt
¼ bunch cilantro
¾ cup (170ml) water

PICO DE GALLO
6 Roma tomatoes
1 red onion
1 bunch cilantro
1 jalapeño pepper, seeded and minced (optional)
2 limes
1 ½ tbsp (23g) salt

1 pint (450g) sour cream
8 (12" [30.5cm]) flour tortillas
2 lb (907g) Monterey Jack and Cheddar cheese blend

To make the carne asada, pat the sirloin steak dry and season with salt. Lightly dust both sides with light and dark chili powders. Marinate, covered, in the refrigerator for at least 6 hours or overnight.

While steaks marinate, make the glaze. Blend all the ingredients in a food processor to a sauce-like consistency. Set aside.

To make the avocado garlic sauce, blend all the ingredients in a food processor until smooth. Pour into a squirt bottle. Mix water with sour cream until it's smooth enough to pour into another squirt bottle.

To make the pico de gallo, dice the tomatoes and red onion. Be sure to finely dice the red onion to minimize its spicy characteristics. Rinse the cilantro and finely mince just the leaves. Add the jalapeño to the mix if you want to heat things up. Combine all the ingredients in a bowl and mix well. Refrigerate the salsa and use the same day.

Remove the steak from the refrigerator and grill in a nonstick skillet over medium-high heat until medium-rare, roughly 4 to 6 minutes on each side. Once the steak has cooled enough to handle, chop into small ¼-inch (6mm) cubes. Add the chopped steak to a nonstick skillet along with the glaze and sauté over high heat for 2 to 3 minutes, until the steak is fully cooked and browned.

To assemble the quesadillas, mix water with the sour cream until it's smooth enough to pour into a squirt bottle. Toast one side of the tortillas in a skillet over medium-low heat until slightly golden brown. Remove from the heat. On half of the toasted side, lay the carne asada meat along with the pico de gallo and a nice handful of shredded cheese. Squirt a generous amount of avocado garlic sauce and sour cream on both sides. Fold the top of the tortilla over and toast the untoasted sides in the skillet over medium-low heat for 1 to 3 minutes on each side, or until the cheese is nicely gooey inside.

Chop into 1-inch (2.5cm) strips on a cutting board and serve with extra avocado garlic sauce on the side.

VENEZUELAN AREPAS WITH MUCHACHO

LA COCINITA FOOD TRUCK—CHEF BENOIT ANGULO—NEW ORLEANS, LA

MAKES 10 TO 12 AREPAS

Where Benoit Angulo grew up in Venezuela, there was an evocatively named street called Calle Hambre, which translates literally to "Hunger Street." Lined with food carts, it was a street familiar to Benoit and his fellow late-night workers as THE place to go to fill their bellies with the big, bold flavors of Venezuelan cuisine after a hard day's work. Chef Benoit Angulo and Rachel Billow hope their food truck, La Cocinita, brings the spirit of Calle Hambre to New Orleans with offerings like these arepas. Benoit claims to have a "muscle memory" of making these. To him, the aromatic brisket, flavored with Malta, wine, and savory spices, is intrinsically linked to childhood, home and comfort. "It's one of those things I crave," he says.

AREPAS
1 ½ tsp (7ml) vegetable oil
1 ½ tsp (8g) salt
2 cups (473ml) warm water
½ lb (227g) fresh masa

CARNE ASADA SEASONING
½ cup (121g) kosher salt
2 tbsp (30g) oregano
1 tbsp (15g) garlic powder
1 tbsp (7g) cumin
1 tbsp (15g) onion powder
1 tbsp (15g) black pepper
1 tsp curry powder

MUCHACHO (VENEZUELAN BRISKET)
2 ½ lb (1134g) beef brisket
1 tbsp (15g) Carne Asada Seasoning (see recipe above)
1 tbsp (13ml) canola oil
1 cup (151g) roughly chopped white onion
½ cup (76g) roughly chopped celery
½ cup (76g) roughly chopped green bell pepper

1 tbsp (10g) minced garlic
2 tbsp (29g) unsalted butter
2 tbsp (30g) salt
1 tbsp (15g) black pepper
1 tbsp (15ml) Worcestershire sauce
1 cup (237ml) red wine (Cabernet or Shiraz, something good enough to drink)
2 bay leaves
1 ½ cups (355ml) beef stock
1 cup (235ml) Malta (Latin American soda flavored with molasses, found in most Hispanic grocery stores)

GUASACACA (VENEZUELAN GUACAMOLE)
2 avocados
¼ bunch cilantro
½ cup (76g) diced green bell pepper
½ cup (76g) diced white onion
¼ cup (60ml) canola oil
2 tbsp (30ml) white vinegar
¼ tsp black pepper
¼ tsp salt

PURPLE CABBAGE SLAW

¼ bunch cilantro, chopped

⅛ medium white onion, chopped

1 ½ tsp (7ml) lime juice

1 ½ tsp (7ml) canola oil

½ tsp yellow mustard

½ tsp mayonnaise

Salt to taste

½ head purple cabbage, shredded

Queso fresco, for garnish

To make the arepas, in a large bowl, combine the oil and salt with the warm water until the salt dissolves. In small increments, slowly add the masa to the water, kneading until smooth and lump-free. Continue until you've mixed in all the masa. Form the masa mixture into patties about 3 inches (7.5cm) in diameter and ¾ inch (2cm) thick, ensuring that the edges are smooth and free of cracks.

Preheat a griddle over medium heat and cook the arepas for 5 to 6 minutes on each side, until light golden brown and slightly crispy on the outside.

To make the carne asada seasoning, combine all the ingredients in a small bowl.

To make the brisket, remove excess fat and silver skin from the meat. Season the brisket with the carne asada seasoning and let it rest at room temperature for at least 30 minutes. Add the canola oil to a deep pan and sear the meat on all sides until medium brown in color. Remove the meat from the pan and let it rest for 30 minutes.

Add the onion, celery, green bell pepper, garlic and butter to the pan, and season with salt and pepper. Lower the heat to medium-low and sweat the veggies until brown bits come off the bottom of the pan. Add the Worcestershire sauce, wine and bay leaves. Bring to a boil and simmer the sauce for 30 minutes.

Preheat the oven to 350°F (180°C, or gas mark 4). Put meat in a deep pan with the sauce. Tightly cover with aluminum foil and bake for 1 hour. Add the beef stock and Malta and bake for another 2 hours. Remove the meat from the oven and let it cool enough to handle. Slice the meat against the grain into 1-inch (2.5cm) slices. Add the meat back to the pan with the sauce and cook for an additional hour.

To make the guasacaca, add all the ingredients to a blender. Puree until smooth. Set aside.

To make the cabbage slaw, blend the cilantro, onion, lime juice, canola oil, mustard, mayonnaise and salt into a dressing. Place the shredded cabbage in a medium bowl. Add the dressing, incrementally, to the cabbage mixture and toss well to combine. Dress to taste.

Cut each arepa to form a pocket. Stuff each one with about 3 ounces (84g) of brisket, then garnish with 1 tablespoon (15ml) of guasacaca, a bit of cabbage slaw, and a sprinkle of queso fresco.

SPICED SPARERIBS WITH CHIMICHURRI SAUCE

THRIVE: SAUCE AND BOWLS—ERIKA REAGOR—PORTLAND, OR

SERVES 6

It's not surprising the dishes coming out of Thrive are focused on fresh and healthy. Head chef Erika Reagor has a keen interest in yoga and a desire to make flavorful food without sacrificing nutrition for convenience. Many of Thrive's eclectic dishes are inspired by international cuisine. This particular dish echoes Argentinean flavors with spareribs braised in beer and served with a bright chimichurri sauce.

SPARERIBS

½ cup (101g) packed brown sugar

2 tbsp (14g) smoked paprika

1 tbsp (8g) fresh toasted cumin seeds, ground

1 tsp red pepper flakes

2 to 3 tbsp (30 to 45g) kosher salt

1 tsp finely ground black pepper

4 lb (1.8kg) pork spareribs

1 or 2 (12-oz [340ml]) bottles amber or porter-style beer

CHIMICHURRI SAUCE

½ cup (20g) parsley leaves

2 tbsp (5g) fresh oregano

6 cloves garlic

1 tsp red pepper flakes

¼ cup (59ml) red wine vinegar

⅓ cup (79ml) grapeseed oil

Sea salt to taste

Preheat the oven to 275°F (140°C, or gas mark 1).

To make the spareribs, combine the brown sugar, smoked paprika, cumin seeds, red pepper flakes, salt and pepper in a bowl and then rub over the ribs. Let sit for 10 minutes. Pour the beer into a roasting pan and place the ribs on top.

Braise the ribs, uncovered, for 3 to 4 hours, or until they are fork-tender and fall away from the bone. Add more beer if the pan becomes dry. Remove from the oven and let rest for 15 to 20 minutes.

To make the chimichurri sauce, combine the herbs, garlic and pepper flakes in a food processor and pulse into a rough chop. Add the vinegar and pulse a few more times. Pour into a bowl. In a thin stream, whisk in the grapeseed oil. Season with salt and let marinate for 1 to 2 hours.

Serve the chimichurri atop the ribs. For a complete meal, enjoy with sautéed vegetables and brown rice.

BRISKET BARBACOA EMPANADA

TACO MONDO—MICHAEL SULTAN AND CAROLYN NGUYEN—PHILADELPHIA, PA

SERVES 6 TO 8

Michael Sultan credits his time as a caterer for his strong organizational skills and love of food made from scratch. Since the age of twenty-two, he's worked for high-end caterers (we're talking $15,000 for twenty guests), gaining experience in cuisines of every style and ethnicity imaginable. He brings that versatility to his food truck, where the menu changes on a weekly basis. These empanadas feature a flavorful brisket in adobo sauce wrapped in flaky dough. "I love barbacoa," he says. "It has this umami-type flavor. It just hits you."

BRINE

¾ cup (181g) kosher salt
½ cup (96g) sugar
¼ cup (60g) granulated garlic
4 qt (3.7l) water

3- to 4-lb (1.4 to 1.8kg) brisket
Salt and pepper
1 (14.5 oz [410ml]) can beef or chicken stock

EMPANADA DOUGH

2 ¼ cups (270g) all-purpose flour
1 ½ tsp (8g) salt
½ cup (112g) unsalted butter, cut into small pieces
1 egg
⅓ cup (79ml) ice water
1 tbsp (15ml) white vinegar

ADOBO SEASONING

1 tbsp (7g) chili powder
1 tbsp (7g) cumin
1 tbsp (15g) granulated garlic

1 tbsp (7g) onion powder
1 tbsp (7g) dry oregano
1 tbsp (7g) smoked paprika
1 ½ tsp (8g) red pepper flakes
2 tbsp (30g) kosher salt
1 tbsp (15g) freshly ground black pepper
1 ½ tsp (4g) ground cinnamon

FILLING

5 tomatoes, diced
1 red onion, diced
1 white onion, diced
1 head garlic, smashed
2 jalapeño pepper, seeded
2 tbsp (30ml) vegetable oil

2 tbsp (30ml) canola oil
1 cup (237ml) heavy cream
2 to 3 cups (241 to 362g) shredded Mexican Chihuahua cheese or fontina
1 egg, beaten
Vegetable oil, if frying

To make the brine, place all the brine ingredients in a pot and bring to a boil. Remove from the heat, let cool, then pour over the brisket in a baking dish or Dutch oven. Cover and refrigerate for 24 hours.

Preheat the oven to 400°F (200°C, or gas mark 6). Remove the brisket from the brine and pat dry. Season with salt and pepper and place in a roasting pan. Place the brisket on the center rack and roast for 20 to 30 minutes or until brown. Remove from the oven and drain off the fat. Lower the temperature to 350°F (180°C, or gas mark 4). Pour the beef stock three-fourths of the way up the brisket. Tuck a piece of parchment paper around the brisket, then cover the pan with aluminum foil and place back in the oven. Braise for approximately 3 hours, or until a knife goes into the meat with little to no resistance. Remove form the oven, discard the parchment, let cool, cover and place in the refrigerator overnight. This step allows moisture to be reabsorbed into the meat.

To make the empanada dough, sift the flour and salt into a food processor. Add the butter and pulse together until it resembles coarse meal. Pour the flour mixture into a stand mixer fitted with a paddle attachment. Combine the egg, water and white vinegar, add to the mixer and mix on low speed until the dough comes together and looks shaggy. Add a little more water if it's too dry. Form the dough into a disk, wrap in plastic wrap and refrigerate for 20 minutes.

To make the adobo seasoning, mix all the ingredients in a bowl. Set aside.

To make the filling, preheat the oven to 350°F (180°C, or gas mark 4). Combine the tomatoes, onions, garlic and jalapeños in a bowl. Lightly coat with vegetable oil and sprinkle in the adobo seasoning. Spread on a cookie sheet lined with parchment and roast in the oven until brown and caramelized. Remove the filling from the oven and blend in a food processor until smooth.

Add the canola oil to a large sauté pan over medium heat. Once the pan is hot, pour in the filling puree and let simmer for 1 minute, and then add the heavy cream. Remove the brisket from the refrigerator and trim off the excess fat. Chop the brisket and add to the simmering liquid. Let the brisket simmer for about 20 minutes, until it shreds apart. Taste for seasoning. Remove the filling from heat and let cool. Add the cheese and stir to combine.

To assemble the empanadas, lightly flour a work surface and roll the dough to ⅛ inch (3mm) thickness. Cut into large rounds. Brush the beaten egg on one side of the round and add a spoonful of the filling. Fold the sides over and press together to seal.

Once sealed you can either bake or fry. If baking, bake at 375°F (190°C, or gas mark 5) for 15 minutes. If frying, bring the oil to 375°F (190°C) and fry until golden brown. To freeze, sprinkle the empanadas with cornmeal and wrap individually with cut pieces of parchment.

CHAPTER 6

KEEPIN' IT REAL: ASIAN

It was an interesting transition moving from Los Angeles to Portland, Oregon. Aside from having to learn how to scrape ice off my windshield in the winter mornings, one of the biggest adjustments for Kim and I was the dearth of available Asian food. We took the abundance of authentic Asian food in LA for granted. We were sometimes shocked when we would hang out with friends who had never tried one bite of Korean or Thai food. Even the least adventurous of my friends in LA has had an outing to a Korean barbecue joint.

At first it was hard for us to find authentic Asian restaurants. It turns out we were looking in the wrong place. We found that the most authentic dishes were actually at food carts. Thai, Korean, Indian, you name it—they were all there on the streets slinging hot and fresh food. And when any of our PDX friends are excited to tell us they finally tried Asian cuisine for the first time, they frequently say it was from a food cart.

If there's one type of food that translates well into food carts and trucks, it's Asian food. Walk around any city in Asia and you'll find an abundance of street food. Food carts like Nong's Khao Man Gai (Thai) in Portland or Parantha Alley (Indian) in New York fill an important gap in each of their respective cities. These cart owners are as real as they come. They're right there in front of you with no barriers, cooking up something authentic for you to try for the first time. You'll find recipes like Nong's Khao Kha Muu or Love Balls' Garlic Yaki Onigiri to fill that gap in your own home.

KAMI (KOREAN AMERICAN MENUS INSPIRED)—JIN JANG

PHILADELPHIA, PENNSYLVANIA

"I just love food," an exuberant Jin Jang says of her decision to work in the food industry. "You can offer all the money in the world or really great food, and I would pick the food. It just makes me so happy." Jin's food truck, KAMI, serves authentic Korean dishes in the University City neighborhood of Philadelphia. Open since October 2012, KAMI specializes in dishes such as bulgogi beef and udon noodles. Her bright red truck has since become a destination point for city dwellers and Drexel University students alike.

Jin strives to provide authentic Korean flavors at affordable prices. While there are plenty of Korean restaurants in Philadelphia, Jin had a difficult time finding any that didn't follow the trend of heavily Americanizing the more traditional dishes. KAMI fills this niche by keeping the flavors of her meats and dishes as close as possible to those of her home country. "I really like the flavors of regular, traditional Korean, so all of my meats are very traditionally flavored. The only Americanized part about my menu is putting it in a cheesesteak."

Jin has grown up making Korean food. Born in Korea, she immigrated to the United States at the age of eight with her mother and sister. "My dad was still overseas in Korea, so my mom had to work all the time," Jin recalls. "I would ask my mom how to cook simple things, like kimchi stew. I started cooking dinner for my little sister and mom before she got back from work." Jin realized she loved the act of preparing meals for her family and eventually graduated to more complex dishes. Eventually, at the age of sixteen, she landed her first job at a restaurant and hasn't left the food scene since.

Although most chefs share the dream of opening up a brick-and-mortar restaurant, the low overhead, speed of production, and superior quality control of a food truck is just too good of an opportunity to pass up. But it's not all about the bottom line. "There are people who want to make good food just for the money. I just want something homier. I want more loving and caring to go into the food."

SOONDUBU STEW

KAMI (KOREAN AMERICAN MENUS INSPIRED)—JANG FAMILY RECIPE—PHILADELPHIA, PA

SERVES 1 OR 2

Soondubu is a traditional Korean soft tofu stew made with varying ingredients. KAMI's has pork and shiitake mushrooms, but feel free to use beef or a variety of seafood (clams, shrimp, oysters, mussels). It's perfect for partaking with friends and family on a cold day. "When I think of Korean recipes, it reminds me of family," says Jin Jang. "I want people to see this recipe as something they can do together with family. That's the Korean culture: you have one big pot, and everyone sits together around the table and shares it."

1 cup (220g) shredded pork shoulder

1 ½ tsp (7ml) sesame oil

1 tbsp (10g) minced garlic

1 tbsp (7g) Korean coarse red pepper powder (add more if you like to be spicier)

¼ cup (17g) sliced shiitake or button mushrooms

¼ cup (38g) diced onion

¼ cup (38g) diced zucchini

1 cup (237ml) vegetable stock

1 (14-oz [396g]) package soft tofu

Salt to season

1 long hot pepper, seeded and diced

½ cup (25g) diced scallion

In a medium pot, mix the pork, sesame oil, garlic and red pepper powder with no heat. Once mixed, turn the heat on high and sauté the mixture for 2 to 4 minutes, until the pork gets some color. Add the mushrooms, onion and zucchini, and then the stock. Bring to a boil and add the tofu. Do not stir often to avoid breaking up the soft tofu.

Lower the heat to a simmer and cook for about 10 minutes. Season to taste with salt. Add the long hot pepper and the scallion just before serving.

Enjoy it with a bowl of rice and a side of kimchi.

ADOBONG PUSIT

LUMPIA SHACK—CHEF NEIL SYHAM—BROOKLYN, NY

SERVES 3 OR 4

Born in the Philippines, dynamic duo Neil Syham and Angie Roca grew up on the sweet, salty, tart and spicy flavors of Filipino cuisine. So it stands to reason that adobo, the national dish of the Philippines, would be a frequent star of Lumpia Shack's menu. "Adobo is based off soy, vinegar, bay leaf and black peppercorns," explains Neil. "You can adobo anything." While it's usually chicken or pork that's being "adoboed," Neil chooses to use squid, another common Filipino ingredient, to give this recipe a rich seafood flavor. Serve over garlic rice with a fried egg.

2 lb (907g) squid

3 tbsp (45ml) oil

4 cloves garlic, crushed

4 bay leaves

½ tsp salt, or to taste

½ tsp pepper, or to taste

1 tsp black peppercorns

¾ cup (177ml) white or coconut vinegar

¾ cup (177ml) fish or chicken stock

1 tbsp (12g) sugar

¼ cup (59ml) soy sauce

1 tsp minced red chiles

1 tsp minced parsley

Detach the head of the squid from the body. Remove the beak and ink sacks and clean the squid under running water.

In a sauté pan over medium heat, add the oil and sauté the garlic until golden brown, 1 to 2 minutes. Add the squid, bay leaves, salt, pepper and peppercorns and sauté for 2 minutes.

Pour in the vinegar, stock, sugar and soy sauce. Bring to a boil over high heat and then reduce to a simmer and cover. Simmer for 45 minutes, or until the squid is fork-tender.

Just before serving, add the minced red chiles and parsley. Eat alone or serve over garlic rice with a fried egg.

JAPANESE CURRY WITH CHICKEN KARA-AGE

JAPACURRY—JAY HAMADA—SAN FRANCISCO, CA

SERVES 8

Curry is to the Japanese what mac and cheese is to Americans: hearty, soothing and one of the most popular dishes in Japan. It's guaranteed at least a weekly spot at the table. With the lack of Japanese food trucks in the Bay Area, Jay Hamada realized he could tap into a culinary need. He briefly toyed with the idea of ramen (going so far as to go to ramen school in Japan), but ultimately decided to go with fast, easy, delicious curry. He says one of the secrets of his curry is going heavy on the onions, which perfectly complements his Japanese fried chicken.

CHICKEN KARA-AGE

2 tbsp (30ml) soy sauce

2 tbsp (30ml) sake

1 tsp grated ginger

1 tsp grated garlic

1 egg yolk

Salt and pepper to taste

1 lb (454g) chicken thighs, cut into 1" to 2" (2.5 to 5cm) cubes

1 cup (99g) flour

1 cup (170g) potato starch

½ tsp black pepper

¼ tsp cayenne pepper

Vegetable oil, for frying

JAPANESE CURRY

2 tbsp (30ml) vegetable oil

2 medium onions, chopped

2 carrots, chopped

2 tbsp (29g) butter

1 tbsp (10g) grated garlic

6 cups (1420ml) water

7 oz (196g) Japanese curry cubes

Cooked rice, for serving

Cayenne pepper, for garnish

To make the kara-age, in a baking dish, combine the soy sauce, sake, ginger, garlic and egg yolk and season with salt and pepper. Add the chicken, cover and marinate for at least 1 hour in the refrigerator. Remove from the marinade, discarding the marinade.

In a bowl, mix the flour, potato starch, black pepper and cayenne pepper. Dip the chicken and coat thoroughly.

Pour vegetable oil into a deep pot or fryer to a depth of 4 to 5 inches (10–12.5cm). Heat to 350°F (177°C) on a deep-fat thermometer. Fry the chicken for 8 minutes, drain and set aside.

To make the curry, heat the oil in a large saucepan over medium heat. Add the chopped onions, carrots, butter and grated garlic and cook, stirring, for 8 to 10 minutes, until the onions brown. Add the water and simmer for about 30 minutes, until you can pass a fork through the carrots. Skim off any oil or foam.

Decrease the heat to low, add the Japanese curry cubes, and stir for 5 to 7 minutes, until the curry becomes thick. Serve the curry over rice with the chicken kara-age. Dust with cayenne pepper for additional heat.

PORK BELLY AND PINEAPPLE ADOBO

THE HERBAN LEGEND MOBILE CAFÉ—BRIAN SEELEY—CHARLOTTE, NC

SERVES 10 TO 12

Chef Brian Seeley of The Herban Legend Mobile Café draws on a love of travel and experiences of international flavors for his menu of eclectic American and international comfort food. This recipe has a particularly sentimental spot in Brian's heart. He met his fiancée in the Middle East, where she cooked adobo for him. "The first time I had it, I loved it," he recalls. Later, in the States this Pork Belly and Pineapple Adobo recipe won him a competition with its rich, tropical flavors.

---

1 cup (237ml) Filipino palm vinegar

2 cups (473ml) toyomansi (Filipino soy sauce with calamansi lime juice)

1 ¼ cups (300ml) water

2 tsp (10g) black pepper

1 medium onion, finely diced

6 cloves garlic, chopped

2 jalapeño peppers, seeded and finely diced

1 can diced pineapple, juice reserved

½ can Sprite

4 lb (1.8kg) pork belly (2 slabs) or pork bull

½ cup (76g) cornstarch

Jasmine rice, for serving

Combine the vinegar, toyomansi, 1 cup (235ml) of the water, black pepper, onion, garlic, jalapeño, pineapple and juice, and Sprite in a bowl. Add the pork, turning to coat, cover and marinate the pork overnight in the refrigerator.

The next day, remove the pork from the marinade and sear in a hot pan until brown on both sides. Cover with the marinade and heat on high just until it starts to bubble. Lower the heat enough to just keep bubbles. Cook at this temperature for 4 hours.

Remove the pork and allow to cool. Cut into 3-inch (7.5cm) strips and slice ¼ inch (6mm) thick.

Meanwhile, bring the marinade to a rolling boil over medium-high heat. Make a slurry of the cornstarch and remaining ¼ cup (60ml) of water, pour into the marinade and cook until the sauce thickens to a gravy-like consistency.

To serve, sear the pieces of pork belly until crisp on both sides. Lay over jasmine rice and top with the sauce.

KHAO KHA MUU

NONG'S KHAO MAN GAI—NONG POONSUKWATTANA—PORTLAND, OR

SERVES 2

Quality, quality, quality. That's what Nong Poonsukwattana is all about. A passionate and determined woman from Thailand, she learned to cook in her mother's restaurant. True to her Thai roots, she keeps her dishes at Nong's Khao Man Gai simple, but made with the utmost attention to detail. In fact, she gained her fame and devoted following by making one dish and one dish only (chicken and rice). Her cart became such a success that she branched out to other dishes, such as these pork hocks, and is selling her Khao Man Gai Sauce in retail locations. These pork hocks are braised in a fragrant, rich, slightly sweet broth and finished with a 6-minute egg and Chinese broccoli.

3 medium eggs

CHILE VINEGAR

2 cloves garlic

1 fresh Thai chile

1 tsp sugar

½ tsp salt

½ cup (118ml) Thai vinegar, preferably Golden Mountain brand

PORK HOCK

2 tbsp (30g) salt

1 tbsp (9g) white pepper

4 cloves garlic

1 cilantro root

1 piece cinnamon

3 pieces star anise

1 pork hock, about 3 lb (1361g)

1 (2l) bottle Coca-Cola

3 dried shiitake mushrooms

½ cup (125ml) oyster sauce, preferably Maekrua brand

1 bunch Chinese broccoli

½ cup (90g) pickled mustard greens, for serving

Steamed jasmine rice, for serving

Fresh cilantro sprigs, for garnish

Bring enough water to cover the 3 eggs comfortably to a boil in a saucepot. Using a thumbtack, poke a hole in each of the eggs. This will prevent them from cracking as they touch the boiling water. Set a timer for 6 minutes and add the eggs to the boiling water. After 6 minutes, shut off the heat and let the eggs sit in the water for exactly 3 minutes. Immediately transfer to an ice water bath. Peel and reserve.

To make the chile vinegar, mash the garlic, chile, sugar and salt in a mortar and pestle. Add to a bowl along with the vinegar and stir to combine.

To make the pork hock, add 1 tablespoon (15g) of the salt, white pepper, garlic and cilantro root to a mortar and pestle. Mash into a paste and set aside.

Heat a small sauté pan over medium heat. Toast the cinnamon and star anise for 2 to 3 minutes or until aromatic.

Rinse the pork hock under cold running water, then add to a large pot. Add the Coca-Cola, shiitake mushrooms, mashed paste, oyster sauce and toasted cinnamon and star anise. Bring to a boil over high heat, then reduce to a low simmer. Simmer for 3 hours, or until the meat easily peels off the bones while still holding its structure.

Taste the broth and check for seasoning. It should taste rich, salty and mildly sweet. Add the remaining 1 tablespoon (15g) salt if needed. Finish by adding the Chinese broccoli and 6-minute eggs to the pot.

Serve with the chile vinegar, pickled mustard greens, steamed jasmine rice and fresh cilantro sprigs.

BUTA KIMCHI

LOVE BALLS BUS—SAO AND GABE ROTHSCHILD—AUSTIN, TX

MAKES 4

Gabe Rothschild and his wife Sao feel Love Balls "embodies the spirit of what we've always wanted to have. It's a comfortable, fun place where we try to get to know most of our customers and provide a unique experience. It's a fun, funky, place." With just a handful of ingredients, this Japanese interpretation of a Korean standard combines pork belly with kimchi for a spicy, meaty treat. (Fun fact: *buta* is Japanese for "pork.") Serve over white rice.

---

1 lb (454g) pork belly

1 tsp salt

4 cups (1363g) chopped kimchi

1 ½ tbsp (22g) gochujang (Korean red chili paste)

1 ½ tbsp (22ml) soy sauce

Thinly slice and chop the pork belly into ½-inch (1.3cm) pieces. Spread out the pieces on a cutting board and lightly salt. Let the pork belly sit for 5 minutes.

Heat a large frying pan over medium-low heat. Add the pork belly and stir for approximately 10 minutes, allowing all sides to slowly brown. When the pork is cooked through, remove from the pan.

Keeping the pork belly oils in the pan, add the kimchi, gochujang and soy sauce. Be sure to include a good amount of the kimchi juices. Once the sauce begins to bubble, reduce the heat to low, cover and allow to simmer for 10 minutes. Stir the pork belly back in and let cook for another few minutes for the flavors to mix.

GARLIC YAKI ONIGIRI

LOVE BALLS BUS—SAO AND GABE ROTHSCHILD—AUSTIN, TX

MAKES 9 RICE BALLS

Gabe Rothschild traveled to Japan for the sole purpose of meeting people and eating good food. While there, he worked on farms in exchange for room and board. In addition to some great experiences, he returned to the States with an appreciation for traditional, home-style cooking found in Japan's countryside, like this Garlic Yaki Onigiri. These fried rice balls have a golden sear so they have a "crisp crunch on the outside and a warm, gooey center. They're simple and savory and a favorite of regulars at Love Balls," says Gabe.

4 cups (842g) uncooked short-grain rice

Vegetable oil

1 tbsp (15g) garlic powder

1 cup (237ml) soy sauce

3 sheets yaki nori (roasted seaweed), cut lengthwise into thirds

Using a rice cooker or stove-top method, rinse and cook the rice. Aerate the rice by stirring with a paddle and let cool slightly. Rice balls are easiest to form when the rice is hot. (But this is also when hands are most often burned.) When the rice is at a manageable temperature, wet your hands in ice water and paddle about 1 cup (235g) of rice into your hand.

Using both hands, form the rice into a triangle. Make the rice triangle firm, rewetting your hands if necessary. Set the onigiri aside on a foiled tray and repeat until all the rice is used (you should get 9 pieces). Place in the refrigerator and let cool for 40 minutes. This allows the rice to congeal and makes for reliable searing.

Coat a large frying pan with vegetable oil over high heat. Place the onigiri in the pan and cook on each side for 5 minutes, or until golden brown.

Combine the garlic powder and soy sauce in a bowl, then pour over the onigiri in the pan; use less for light flavor or more for those desiring something salty. Let the soy sauce reduce and sear one side for 5 to 10 seconds, until it caramelizes, then using tongs, flip and sear the opposite side. Remove from the pan and place each onigiri facedown on the yaki nori strips. Wrap the seaweed around the onigiri and enjoy!

CARROT AND COCONUT PARANTHAS

PARANTHA ALLEY—RAJEEV YERNENI AND RETU SINGLA—NEW YORK, NY

MAKES 10 PARANTHAS

Paranthas are a stuffed fry bread as common in India as pancakes are here. This versatile food can be stuffed with just about anything from sweet to savory (in fact, a common Indian practice is to take leftovers from the night before and roll them into a parantha). In this recipe, Retu Singla and Rajeev Yerneni choose to stuff their paranthas with a fragrant mixture of carrots, coconut and spices. "You can't skimp on the stuffing," advises Retu. "And when you roll out the parantha, you want to try to make it a certain level of thinness. You need to have really nice grill marks, a nice brown. If you do that, then when you eat it, it'll be crispy on the outside and really soft on the inside."

CARROT AND COCONUT STUFFING

1 tbsp (13ml) olive oil

½ tsp mustard seeds

½ tsp methi (fenugreek) seeds

½ tsp cumin seeds

1 sprig curry leaves

2 or 3 green chiles, seeded and chopped

½ tsp urad dal

½ tsp chana dal

½" (1.3cm) piece ginger, grated

2 cloves garlic, grated

4 carrots, peeled and shredded

1 cup (76g) shredded unsweetened coconut

½ tsp red pepper flakes

Salt to taste

PARANTHAS

3 cups (390g) atta (whole wheat chapati flour)

1 cup (237ml) water

1 tbsp (13ml) olive oil, plus more for frying

To make the carrot and coconut stuffing, heat the olive oil in a pan over medium heat. Once hot, add the mustard seeds, methi and cumin seeds, curry leaves, green chiles, urad dal and chana dal, ginger and garlic. Sauté for 5 to 6 seconds. Add the chopped carrots and mix well.

Cook with the lid on over medium heat for 4 to 5 minutes, stirring occasionally. Reduce the heat and add the coconut, red pepper flakes and salt to taste. Cook uncovered for about 10 minutes, until the carrots are slightly soft, stirring occasionally. Turn off the heat and place in a mixing bowl.

To make the paranthas, in a bowl, mix 2 cups (260g) of the atta flour and the water until a dough forms. Add the olive oil and knead until the dough is well mixed. Separate the dough into large balls approximately the size of golf balls. Roll between your palms, applying gentle pressure, until the balls are smooth and without cracks.

Spread the remaining 1 cup (130g) atta flour on a small plate. Press the dough balls gently, flattening them into the dry flour, coating both sides. Roll out the dough into 4-inch (10cm) disks.

Place a spoonful of stuffing in the center of each disk. Gather the sides of the disk up and over the filling, making a stuffed dough ball. Press gently onto the atta flour on both sides.

Roll out the stuffed dough ball to about ⅛ inch (5mm) thick. If the dough becomes sticky from the stuffing oozing out, add more atta flour.

Add a spoonful of olive oil to a pan. Add a dough ball and cook on one side over high heat for 2 to 3 minutes, until golden, then flip and cook on the other side until golden.

THAI GREEN CURRY BREAKFAST BOWL WITH BASIL CHICKEN

GAI GAI THAI—KRIS PETCHARAWISES—MINNEAPOLIS, MN

SERVES 4 TO 6

Kris Petcharawises wanted a change. Weary of the journalism world, he realized it was time for a new career path. His food stand, Gai Gai Thai serves authentic, classic Thai flavors that Kris grew up with while steering away from the usual clichéd Thai-American dishes. This breakfast bowl, for example, combines all the flavors readily found in Thai cuisine—sweet curry, salty fish sauce, spicy chilies and fragrant basil. "It's kind of like an inside joke," says Kris. "Because there's no breakfast for Thai people. They eat 24/7, it's like a sport and Thais are really good at it. But we needed something to sell for the breakfast crowd. This dish is really representative of Thai food."

2 cups (421g) uncooked jasmine rice

CURRY SAUCE
1 (403ml) can coconut cream or coconut milk
2 oz (55g) green curry paste
2 tbsp (24g) palm or white sugar
1 tbsp (15g) fish sauce

CARROT SLAW
6–8 garlic cloves
8–10 Thai chilies
4 tbsp (59g) fish sauce
1–2 limes, juiced
1–2 tbsp (13-26g) vegetable oil
2 cups (99g) sliced carrots

BASIL CHICKEN
1 pound (454g) free-range ground chicken or turkey
3 tbsp (44g) sweet soy sauce
2 tbsp (30g) fish sauce
½ cup (118ml) vegetable oil
1 cup (40g) sweet Thai basil leaves

THAI OMELETTE
3–4 eggs
4 tsp (20g) fish sauce
1 tbsp (13g) vegetable oil

½ cup (25g) green onions, garnish
½ cup (75g) crispy fried onions, garnish
½ cup (80g) sliced red peppers, garnish

Start by cooking the rice in a rice cooker or by the directions on the package.

To make the curry sauce, heat the coconut cream and curry paste over medium heat in a small pot for about 5 minutes or until it boils. Stir in the sugar and fish sauce. Bring the mixture back to a boil, about 5 minutes, and let it simmer. The curry sauce will look pale green when done.

For the carrot slaw, pound the garlic and chilies with a mortar and pestle into a paste, or use a food processor. Use half of the garlic and chili paste (the other half will be for the basil chicken) and add the fish sauce, lime juice, vegetable oil and carrots.

To make the basil chicken, mix the soy sauce and fish sauce. Sauté the garlic-chili paste in a frying pan on medium heat for 1 to 2 minutes. Add the chicken, soy sauce, oil and fish sauce and cook for about 5 minutes until there is no pink in the chicken. Once the chicken is done cooking, add the basil leaves. Set aside and cover until ready to serve.

For the Thai omelette, beat the eggs with the fish sauce. With a frying pan on medium-high heat, lightly oil the pan with the oil. Once the pan is hot, add the egg mixture and fry each side of the omelette for about 10 seconds or until each side is golden and crispy.

Assemble the bowl by starting with the jasmine rice on the bottom. Top the rice with sections of the basil chicken, Thai omelette and the carrot slaw. Pour the green curry sauce over the chicken and omelette. Garnish with green onions, fried onions and red peppers.

CHAPTER 7

BEST OF BOTH WORLDS: FUSION

There's a lot of pressure on food carts to produce something that people have never seen before. If you haven't stepped foot onto a food cart yet, you should make it a point to do so. You won't get a sense of how amazing it is for chefs to cook in such a small space and sometimes with less equipment than the average household until you're standing inside one. Often, there are no tables at stops and you need to adapt your food to make it easy for customers to eat while standing. Creativity is often bred out of necessity. From this it's easy to see why fusing two ethnic cuisines (such as putting variations of delicious fillings in a burrito or a taco, for example) is only logical.

You can almost define all food as some sort of fusion food. If you look back far enough with any type of food, it probably borrowed another culture's cuisine somewhere down the line. Why not take the best flavors from different cuisines and make something new and fresh? It just makes sense. If there's one dominant trend we've seen in food carts, it's the abundance of fusion menus, specifically Asian fusion cuisine. In this chapter you'll find recipes from carts that infuse their food with spices and flavor profiles from different cuisines into one cohesive dish.

Hawaii is a region rich with Asian influences, so you'll also find some recipes from one of the original fusion cuisines, Hawaiian food. Poi Dog in Philly's Philadelphia Lumpia is a great example of these hybrid treats. Think Philly cheesesteak in an egg roll. You're probably wondering, why didn't I think of that? I'm sure at some point in history somebody thought pairing peanut butter and jelly was a crazy idea. That's what fusion food is all about: eating something you've never had before. Food carts are leading the way.

THE PEACHED TORTILLA—
ERIC SILVERSTEIN
AUSTIN, TEXAS

When Eric Silverstein of The Peached Tortilla graduated from law school, he never in a million years pictured himself running a food truck recognized by Restaurant Hospitality as one of the "Stars of Street Food" in 2012. And yet Eric has quickly built a reputation for himself serving up cuisine that beautifully fuses the bold, decadent flavors of the South with savory Asian tastes.

At the age of twenty-six, Eric found himself at a crossroads: pursuing a lucrative law career that wasn't quite sparking the enthusiasm he craved or opening up a food truck—a relatively unknown business venture that had just started catching on in those days. "I took the leap," he recalls. "I quit my job, moved down to Austin, and opened up two months later."

The cuisine The Peached Tortilla serves up is all based on food that has influenced Eric in some way. Born in Tokyo, he grew up traveling around Asia, Singapore and China, cutting his teeth on Asian flavors. It wasn't until Eric was ten that he was introduced to true Southern-style food in his new home of Atlanta, Georgia. His dishes bring both of these experiences together on a menu where barbecued brisket is just as likely to end up in a taco as Chinese barbecued tofu.

"It's a hard job," he admits. "Food trucks are manual labor. You may be working the grill one day and it's 120 degrees in the kitchen. There are a million things that could go wrong. It's one of the hardest things you can get into, in my opinion. But it's been a wild, crazy ride."

PAD THAI TACO

THE PEACHED TORTILLA—ERIC SILVERSTEIN—AUSTIN, TX

MAKES 4 OR 5 TACOS

Eric Silverstein got this recipe from a line cook who briefly worked for The Peached Tortilla. "He was a really talented guy," he says. "Insane, but talented and obsessed with Asian food." It was his idea to take the basic elements of pad Thai, with its nutty sauce and bright flavors of green onion and lime, and trade the rice noodles for soft corn tortillas. It's a Peached Tortilla twist on a Thai favorite.

CHICKEN MARINADE

3 to 4 lb (1.4 to 1.8kg) boneless, skinless chicken thighs

¼ cup (59ml) rice wine vinegar

¼ cup (40g) minced garlic

¼ cup (59ml) light soy sauce

2 tbsp (31g) chili paste

¼ cup (48g) sugar

PAD THAI VEGGIE MIX

1 cup (66g) sliced mushrooms

1 bunch scallions, chopped

¼ cup (63ml) pad Thai sauce

1 tbsp (26ml) cooking oil

4 eggs

20 (5" [12.5cm]) white corn tortillas

TOPPINGS

1 bunch cilantro, chopped

1 bunch scallions, chopped

¼ cup (40g) chopped peanuts

2 limes, cut into wedges

To make the chicken marinade, combine all the ingredients in a bowl and let rest overnight in the refrigerator. Cook the chicken on an open flame grill or on the stove for 8 to 10 minutes, until cooked through. Once the chicken is cooked and has cooled, dice the meat.

To make the veggie mix, combine the mushrooms, scallions, pad Thai sauce and the oil in a large skillet over medium-high heat. Let the mushrooms and scallions cook through for 2 to 3 minutes, then add the eggs. Scramble the eggs with the veggie mix until the eggs are cooked. After another 2 to 3 minutes, add the diced chicken and stir to combine.

Heat the tortillas up on a griddle or stovetop for 1 minute on each side, then add the pad Thai mix (double up the tortillas if you prefer). Garnish with the cilantro, scallions and peanuts and serve with a lime wedge.

BANH MI TACO

THE PEACHED TORTILLA—ERIC SILVERSTEIN—AUSTIN, TX

MAKES 4 TACOS

Eric Silverstein of The Peached Tortilla has a mission: introduce the bold flavors of his Asian upbringing to his hungry customers of the South. "We wanted to do riffs on traditional foods, but make them more approachable. When we started with the Banh Mi Tacos, a lot of people didn't know what banh mi was." A banh mi is a Vietnamese sandwich usually served up on a fresh baguette, which Eric replaces with soft tortillas. These rich, tangy tacos filled with pork belly and pickled vegetable are the perfect introduction.

RUB

¼ cup (29g) Chinese five-spice powder
¼ cup (50g) packed brown sugar
Kosher salt and black pepper to taste

1 tbsp (13ml) vegetable oil
3 ½ lb (1.6kg) piece of pork belly

BRAISING LIQUID

1 onion, chopped
3 cloves garlic, minced
3 tbsp (47ml) dark soy sauce
¼ cup (59ml) light soy sauce
3 pieces star anise
½ cup (118ml) water
¼ cup (59ml) rice vinegar
½ cup (101g) packed brown sugar

DAIKON AND CARROT SALAD

½ lb (227g) daikon
½ lb (227g) carrot
2 to 3 tbsp (30 to 44ml) rice vinegar
2 tbsp (29ml) chili garlic sauce
1 tbsp (15ml) fish sauce
3 tbsp (36g) granulated sugar

SRIRACHA MAYO

½ cup (110g) mayonnaise
3 tbsp (42g) Sriracha sauce
1 tbsp (15ml) lemon juice
1 tbsp (15ml) rice vinegar

4 (5″ [12.5cm]) tortillas (flour or corn)
Chopped cilantro, for garnish

To make the rub, combine all the ingredients in a small bowl.

Preheat the oven to 350°F (180°C, or gas mark 4).

In a cast-iron skillet, heat the vegetable oil over high heat. Rub the dry rub into the pork belly. Once the pork belly is seasoned, sear it in a skillet for 4 minutes on each side to ensure that you have sealed in the juices. The pork belly should be nicely browned on each side but not burned. Pull the pork belly out of the skillet and let it rest.

To make the braising liquid, without emptying the juices and bits from the skillet, sauté the onion and garlic over medium heat for 2 minutes, until browned. Add the dark soy, light soy, star anise, water, rice vinegar and brown sugar and stir to combine. Add the pork belly. The braising liquid should rise only halfway up the pork belly.

Place the skillet in the oven and let it braise for approximately 3 ½ hours. Pork belly should be very moist and tender and pull apart easily. Remove from the oven, let rest and chop into smaller pieces.

To make the salad, use a mandoline to julienne the daikon and carrot into thin strips. In a bowl, combine the daikon, carrot, rice vinegar, chili garlic sauce, fish sauce and granulated sugar. Let the mixture rest for at least 3 to 4 hours in the refrigerator before use.

For the Sriracha mayo, mix the mayonnaise, Sriracha, lemon juice and rice vinegar together and pour into a squeeze bottle.

Assemble the tacos by heating the tortillas on a griddle or stovetop for 1 minute on each side. Add the pork belly. Top with the daikon and carrot salad and Sriracha mayo and garnish with the cilantro.

CHICKEN AND PUMPKIN SAUTÉ

EAT FUKI—ALEX MEISELS, SEABROOK GUBBINS AND CHEF CRAIG PETERSON—SAN FRANCISCO, CA

SERVES 4

Alex Meisels and Seabrook Gubbins hope to cross culinary boundaries with the flavors of their Eat Fuki food truck. Inspired by the spice routes, Fuki is an amalgamation of Alex and Seabrook's experiences traveling abroad and sampling the flavors of cultures across the globe. "When the spice trade first happened you got a new flavor, a new idea and you incorporated that into your local dishes," explains Seabrook. "I'm sure that was an incredibly exciting time." Seabrook and Alex bring several new ideas together in their spice-laden Chicken and Pumpkin Sauté. Go ahead and have seconds. The best thing about this dish is, even if you eat way too much, you won't feel heavy. "It's somehow savory and rich yet light," says Alex.

CHICKEN AND PUMPKIN SAUTÉ

1 medium whole pumpkin or butternut squash

7 tbsp (105ml) olive oil

1 shallot, diced

3 tsp (10g) sea salt

⅛ tsp cayenne pepper

½ tsp cinnamon

2 tsp (8g) palm sugar or brown sugar

2 Brussels sprouts, thinly shaven

½ bunch scallions

½ medium onion, quartered

6 bay leaves

1 ½ lb (680g) boneless, skinless chicken thighs

1 tsp paprika

2 tsp (5g) cumin

PUMPKIN PAD THAI SAUCE

¾ tbsp (7g) tamarind paste or ¼ cup (59ml) apple cider vinegar

1 cup (237ml) pumpkin stock

¼ cup (50g) palm sugar or brown sugar

½ tsp cornstarch

1 ½ tsp (7g) ginger paste or minced fresh ginger

1 tbsp (3g) cilantro, for garnish

Chopped scallion, for garnish

1 tbsp (10g) roasted sesame seeds, for garnish

Sriracha sauce, for serving

Preheat the oven to 375°F (190°C, or gas mark 5).

To make the sauté, cut the pumpkin in half and scrape out the pulp and seeds into a bowl (do not discard). Break down the pumpkin by cutting it into fourths, then into eighths. Cut off the pumpkin skin (do not discard). Dice the pumpkin into approximately ½-inch (1.3cm) cubes.

In a bowl, toss the cubed pumpkin with 3 tablespoons (45ml) of the olive oil, shallot, 1 teaspoon sea salt, cayenne pepper, cinnamon and palm sugar. Spread on a sheet tray and bake for 15 minutes, or until tender. Remove from the oven, add to a bowl and toss in the Brussels sprouts and scallions to just warm through. Set aside. Do not turn off the oven.

For the pumpkin stock, add 1 tablespoon (15ml) of the olive oil, 1 teaspoon sea salt and the onion to a pot. Sauté for about 1 minute over medium heat. Add the pumpkin skins, pulp and seeds. Fill the pot with cold water until it covers the pumpkin by 1 to 2 inches (2.5 to 5cm). Add the salt and bay leaves and bring to a boil. Reduce the heat and simmer for 1 hour. Strain the pumpkin stock and let cool. There should be enough for 1 cup (235ml) of stock.

Cut the chicken into ½-inch (1.3cm) cubes. Marinate the chicken in the remaining 3 tablespoons (45ml) of olive oil, 1 teaspoon sea salt, cayenne, paprika and cumin for 30 minutes. Spread the chicken cubes on a sheet tray and roast for 10 minutes. Set aside.

To make the sauce, combine the tamarind paste, pumpkin stock, palm sugar and cornstarch in a saucepot and bring to a low boil over medium heat. Add the ginger and stir. Cook for 10 to 20 minutes, until the sauce is reduced by half and then remove from the heat and let cool.

In a bowl, combine the cooked chicken, pumpkin, cilantro and scallion and then plate. Drizzle the pumpkin pad Thai sauce over the chicken and sprinkle with the sesame seeds. Add a little Sriracha to spice it up.

BRAISED COCONUT CHIPOTLE PORK SHOULDER WITH CARROT SLAW

EAT FUKI—ALEX MEISELS, SEABROOK GUBBINS, AND CHEF CRAIG PETERSON—SAN FRANCISCO, CA

SERVES 4

In their desire to discover new combinations of flavor, there was one that Alex Meisels and Seabrook Gubbins never expected to work together well: chipotle and coconut milk. Originally, they had purchased a pork shoulder and chipotle for one recipe, and coconut milk and Asian spices for a second dish. Yet they forgot chicken, a key ingredient for the second. So they just threw it all together, and dang if it wasn't delicious. "Cooking is such a creative process," says Alex. "It's perfect for fusing different flavors from different areas." This is one you'll have to taste to believe.

PORK SHOULDER

1 lb (454g) pork shoulder
1 clove garlic, minced
1 tsp salt
2 tbsp (26ml) vegetable oil
1 to 2 (14-oz [392g]) cans coconut milk
2 tsp (10ml) fish sauce
Sauce from 3-oz (84g) can chipotle in adobo

CARROT SLAW

¼ tsp sugar
½ tsp caraway seed
¼ tsp cumin seed
2 tbsp (30ml) olive oil
½ tsp sweet paprika
1 tsp lemon juice
Pinch of cayenne pepper
2 large carrots, shredded
Salt and pepper to taste

2 tbsp (5g) cilantro, for garnish
Quinoa or rice, for serving

To make the pork, cut the pork shoulder into ½-inch (1.3cm) cubes. In a bowl, mix the pork with the garlic and salt. In a skillet or large pan, heat the oil over medium heat and add the pork. Cook for 3 to 4 minutes, until brown. Transfer the pork to a pot and add enough of the coconut milk to cover. Add the fish sauce and chipotle sauce. Bring the mixture to a slow boil and reduce the heat to a simmer. Cook for 1 to 1 ½ hours, until the pork is tender.

To make the carrot slaw, in a bowl, whisk together the sugar, caraway seed, cumin seed, olive oil, sweet paprika, lemon juice and cayenne pepper. Add the shredded carrots and stir thoroughly; add salt and pepper to taste.

When the pork is done cooking, garnish with the cilantro. Serve over quinoa or rice with a side of carrot slaw.

BACON-WRAPPED HAWAIIAN TERRIER-KI DOG

TOKYO DOGGIE STYLE—CHEF KEITH YOKOYAMA AND ALLIE YAMAMOTO—
LOS ANGELES, CA

MAKES 1 HOT DOG

Allie Yamamoto from Tokyo Doggie Style loves the experience of owning and operating a food truck. "You travel everywhere every day and get to meet different people from different neighborhoods and demographics," she says. "I enjoy it very much." But not as much as the Los Angeles crowd enjoys her and her partner's fusion of Japanese and Southern Californian cuisine. This recipe combines the LA institution of bacon-wrapped street dogs with tangy Japanese condiments, and throws in some sweet pineapple for good measure.

1 all-beef hot dog
1 strip thinly sliced bacon
½ ounce (14g) fresh pineapple
Butter
1 New England–style hot dog bun
Wasabi mayo
Teriyaki sauce
Aonori flakes (seaweed flakes)

Kizami nori (shredded seaweed)

Wrap the all-beef hot dog with a slice of bacon and grill in a pan over high heat for 3 to 4 minutes, until the bacon is cooked on all sides. Cut the pineapple into ¼-inch (6mm) rings. Grill the pineapple rings on both sides and cut into bite-size pieces.

Spread butter on both sides of the hot dog bun and toast for 2 to 3 minutes, until it turns golden brown on both sides.

Place the bacon-wrapped hot dog in the bun with the grilled pineapple on top. In a zigzag motion, drizzle wasabi mayo and then teriyaki sauce. Sprinkle the aonori flakes and kizami nori on top.

SPICY AHI POKE

HULA GIRL TRUCK—MIKALA BRENNAN—WASHINGTON, D.C.

SERVES 2 TO 4

Poke (pronounced POH-kay) is a staple of Hawaiian culture formed by generations of Hawaiian fishermen cutting their fresh catches into cubes and seasoning them with whatever ingredients they had on hand. "Poke is so common in the Hawaiian culture," says Mikala Brennan of Hula Girl. "You can stop at a local grocery store and choose from several freshly made varieties." Mikala uses sashimi-grade ahi tuna and a Japanese red pepper blend.

2 lb (907g) fresh ahi tuna, sashimi grade, diced into bite-size pieces

1 tsp grated ginger

½ cup (118ml) soy sauce

1 to 2 tbsp (15 to 30ml) sesame oil

2 tsp (10g) Hawaiian sea salt or kosher salt

1 tbsp (15ml) chile oil

1 tsp Japanese togarashi or red pepper flakes

½ cup (25g) finely chopped scallion

1 tbsp (15g) furikake or black and white sesame seeds

In a large bowl, combine the ahi tuna and all of the ingredients except the furikake. Mix gently, but well. Cover the bowl and refrigerate for 30 minutes

To serve, re-toss the poke; check the seasonings and adjust if needed. Sprinkle furikake on top before serving.

Serve by itself, with fried wonton chips, or in a lettuce wrap.

BULGOGI FILO BITES

KAMI (KOREAN AMERICAN MENUS INSPIRED)—JANG FAMILY RECIPE—PHILADELPHIA, PA

SERVES 5 OR 6

Jin Jang finds her inspiration in the unlikeliest of places: Korean television. "I watch a lot of dramas," she admits. "That's my relaxation while I'm prepping. I'll have my laptop out. There're certain things I'll see and think, 'Oh yeah, I forgot about those!'" Jin finds ways to incorporate traditional Korean flavors with less common ingredients, such as filo dough. In this recipe, Jin fills golden, flaky sheets of filo dough with bulgogi and, of course, cream cheese.

BULGOGI MARINADE

⅓ cup (79ml) soy sauce

1 tsp garlic puree

1 tbsp (12g) sugar

¼ Asian pear, pureed in a blender

1 tsp sesame oil

1 tsp black pepper

½ lb (227g) rib-eye beef, very thinly sliced

Sliced vegetables, as desired

1 (1-lb [454g]) package filo dough #7

4 tablespoons (60g) butter, melted

Cream cheese to taste

Preheat the oven to 375°F (190°C, or gas mark 5).

To make the marinade, in a bowl, mix all the ingredients for the marinade. Add the beef and mix well. Cover and refrigerate for 30 minutes.

In a frying pan over medium heat, add the marinated beef and cook for about 5 minutes, or until there is no pink in the beef. At this point, feel free to add mushrooms, onions or any other vegetables you might like, even kimchi. Once cooked, set aside and cool.

Cut the filo dough into 1 ½-inch (3.8cm)-wide strips and set aside under a damp towel to keep it from drying out. Take 2 pieces of filo dough; brush one with butter and lay the other piece on top. Place a dollop of cream cheese about 1 inch (2.5cm) away from one end and about 2 tablespoons (30g) of bulgogi on top. Fold the filo dough into a triangular shape by folding a corner of the dough up over the filling until the short edge lines up with the side edge. Continue folding into triangles until there are 2 inches (5cm) left, then brush some butter to seal the remaining length of dough (see photo on page 147).

Place the triangles on a cookie sheet 1 inch (2.5cm) apart. Bake for about 10 to 12 minutes, until light golden brown.

COCONUT-CASHEW KAFFIR LIME TROUT WITH FRESH PINEAPPLE SLAW

CARTE BLANCHE—JESSIE ARON—PORTLAND, OR

SERVES 2

Jessie Aron didn't always think she'd be a chef. She tried her hand attending college, but she felt like something was missing. "I felt like I wasn't learning as much as I wanted to," she says of her college years. "Then I went to cooking school and couldn't stop learning. It was incredible." She continues to learn from the many different regional and ethnic cuisines available today. She absorbs techniques and flavors and infuses them into her adventurous dishes, such as the Coconut-Cashew Kaffir Lime Trout. "It's outrageously aromatic and has a really cool play of unexpected flavors." Jessie prefers the fish to be sautéed in turmeric-infused oil; however, if it's hard to find she recommends substituting 1 ½ tablespoons (22g) of butter or coconut oil, or omitting the oil-infusing step altogether.

CRUST

¼ cup (43g) roasted and salted cashews

¼ cup (19g) baker's sweetened coconut, toasted in the oven at low heat until golden brown

¼ cup (30g) panko

1 tbsp (2g) finely minced kaffir lime leaves (found fresh or frozen in Asian grocery stores)

2 tbsp (19g) nutritional yeast (optional)

1 tbsp (13g) brown sugar

Salt and black pepper to taste

SLAW DRESSING

1 ½ tsp (7ml) fish sauce

2 tsp (8g) brown sugar

2 tsp (10ml) fresh lime juice

1 tbsp (15ml) coconut milk (optional)

1 tsp Sriracha sauce

SLAW

½ cup (90g) medium diced fresh pineapple

½ cup (170g) finely shredded napa cabbage

¼ cup (170g) finely shredded carrot (use a ridged peeler)

TURMERIC-INFUSED OIL

1 small raw turmeric root, cut in half lengthwise (found fresh or frozen in Asian grocery stores)

½ cup (120ml) neutral-flavored oil (basically any oil besides olive oil)

2 (4- to 5-oz [112 to 140g]) fillets of trout or any fish you prefer (salmon, halibut, tilapia and steelhead will work)

2 tbsp (19g) rice flour

2 scallions, sliced into 1" (2.5cm) matchsticks (optional)

1 tbsp (3g) fresh dill, picked off the stem (optional)

1 tbsp (15ml) sweet soy sauce (sometimes called kecap manis, found in Asian markets)

Fresh cilantro and mint, for garnish (optional)

To make the crust, combine the cashews, toasted coconut, panko and minced kaffir lime in a food processor and blend for about 30 seconds until you have a coarse, sandy mixture similar to cookie crumbs. Add the nutritional yeast and brown sugar, and season with salt and pepper to taste.

To make the slaw dressing, combine all the ingredients in a bowl and adjust the levels of salty (fish sauce), sweet (sugar), sour (lime) and spice (Sriracha) to your liking.

To make the slaw, combine the pineapple, napa cabbage and carrot in a large bowl. Just before serving, add the dressing and toss to combine.

To make the turmeric-infused oil, place the raw turmeric and oil in a shallow sauté pan over medium-low heat. Allow the turmeric to sizzle gently for about 10 minutes. Remove from the heat. The oil will be almost neon yellow in color and will take on the aroma of fresh turmeric. When the oil cools, set aside. You will have extra oil for future use.

Dredge trout fillets in the rice flour. Heat 3 tablespoons (45ml) of the turmeric-infused oil in a shallow frying pan over medium-high heat and sauté the scallions and dill until the scallions begin to brown slightly, 1 to 2 minutes. Add the trout to the pan and allow it to develop a nice sear. Be careful, because fish cooks very quickly and this should take about 1 minute or less depending on the thickness of the fillet. Flip the trout and top with the loose and crumbly crust. Reduce the heat to low and drizzle in the sweet soy sauce. Be careful not to burn the crust. Move everything around in the pan with a spatula or tongs. The trout should be done in about another minute.

Pile half of the slaw on top of each fillet. Garnish with cilantro and mint. This dish can be served by itself or with rice, quinoa or your favorite grain.

LOCO MOCO MAZEMEN

POI DOG PHILLY—KIKI ARANITA AND CHRIS VACCA—PHILADELPHIA, PA

SERVES 4

Food cart owners have the unique challenge of providing restaurant-quality food in a space the fraction of the size of a commercial kitchen. Often, these limitations result in chefs getting creative. Kiki Aranita wanted to feature the hamburger patty and fried egg of the Hawaiian Loco Moco but didn't have the grill to do so. Her solution? Mazemen: a Japanese brothless ramen. Her Loco Moco Mazemen is ground beef and a 6-minute egg on a bed of noodles topped with miso gravy. A perfect marriage of Hawaii meets Japan. The *maze* in *mazemen* means "mixed" in Japanese. To get the full experience, be sure to *maze* your noodles.

¾ lb (340g) ground beef

4 eggs

4 ¼ oz (120g) dried ramen noodles

MARINADE

1 tsp grated ginger

2 cloves garlic, grated

⅓ cup (50g) diced white onion

2 tbsp (30ml) shoyu

1 tsp sugar

1 tsp sesame oil

½ tsp black pepper

MISO GRAVY

2 tbsp (29g) butter

⅓ cup (33g) all-purpose flour

2 cups (473ml) beef stock

2 tbsp (29g) white miso

1 tsp (5g) black pepper

Salt to taste

4 tbsp (40g) fried shallots

Pinch of furikake

8 sheets roasted Korean seaweed (about 2" x 3" [5 x 7.5cm]), for garnish (optional)

To make the marinade, combine all the ingredients in a medium bowl. Add the ground beef, cover and marinate in the refrigerator for about 2 hours.

Bring a small pot of water to a boil over high heat, add the eggs and boil for 6 minutes. Drain and immediately dunk in ice water. Peel and set aside.

Cook the ramen noodles according to the package directions, drain and set aside.

To make the gravy, melt the butter in a saucepan over medium heat and stir in the flour. Once the roux browns lightly, 1 to 2 minutes, whisk in the beef stock, then the miso. Add the black pepper and salt to taste. Cook for about 6 minutes until the gravy thickens.

Remove the beef from the refrigerator, add to a skillet set over medium-high heat and sauté until cooked through, 2 to 3 minutes.

Divide the noodles among 4 bowls, dress with the miso gravy, then top evenly with the beef, 1 egg, the fried shallots and furikake. Tuck 2 sheets of seaweed next to the rim of each bowl.

PHILADELPHIA LUMPIA

POI DOG PHILLY—KIKI ARANITA AND CHRIS VACCA—PHILADELPHIA, PA

MAKES 12 LUMPIA

In Hawaii, the term *poi dog* refers to a mixed breed or mutt. Kiki Aranita could not have picked a more fitting name for her food cart, which combines the flavors of her native Hawaii with those of local Philadelphia. She has a unique palate open to a fusion of flavors, like those in her Philadelphia Lumpia, a take on the classic Philly cheesesteak wrapped in a Filipino-style crispy spring roll.

EGG WASH

½ cup (76g) cornstarch

½ cup (118ml) water

2 eggs

LUMPIA

1 tbsp (15ml) canola oil

1 tbsp (14g) butter

1 ½ medium sweet onions, thinly sliced

2 tsp (10g) Kosher salt

Black pepper to taste

1 lb (453g) rib eye, thinly sliced and gristle-free

12 (8" [20cm]) lumpia or spring roll wrappers

½ cup (60g) crumbled sharp provolone cheese

Cornstarch

LONG HOT DIPPING SAUCE

5 long hot peppers, roasted quickly over an open flame and skinned

1 poblano pepper, roasted quickly over an open flame and skinned

½ cup (118ml) white vinegar

2 tbsp (24g) sugar

1 tbsp (15ml) beef stock

2 tbsp (30ml) water

1 ½ tbsp (22ml) lime juice

1 ½ tsp kosher salt

2 cloves garlic

¼ Spanish onion, sautéed

Canola oil, for frying

To make the egg wash, combine all the ingredients in a bowl and beat to combine.

To make the lumpia, in a pan over medium heat, heat the oil and butter, add the onions, ½ teaspoon of the salt and pepper and sauté for 5 minutes, until caramelized. Season the rib eye with salt and pepper to taste. Add to the onions and sauté quickly, 2 to 3 minutes, until browned. Transfer to a plate lined with paper towels to drain. The lumpia filling needs to be dry to prevent it from bursting through the wrapper while frying.

Place 3 tablespoons (45g) of the rib eye and onions along the bottom edge of each lumpia wrapper, leaving room on the left and right sides to fold them over. Place 1 ½ teaspoons (5g) of cheese over the rib eye and onions. Brush the egg wash along the top, left and right edges of the wrapper. Fold the left and right sides on top of the filling and brush the egg wash along their sides. Roll very tightly from the bottom edge to the top. If the lumpia wrapper breaks, start over.

Spread the cornstarch on a plate, roll the lumpia in the cornstarch, and line up on a baking sheet. Place in the freezer for at least 1 hour. Freezing gives them structural integrity.

Meanwhile, make the long hot dipping sauce. Add all the ingredients to a blender and puree until smooth.

When ready to serve, pour the canola oil into a deep pot or fryer to a depth of 4 to 5 inches (10 to 15cm). Heat the oil to 325° to 350°F (163° to 177°C) on a deep-fat thermometer. Add the lumpia in batches, being careful not to crowd the oil, and fry for 4 to 5 minutes, until crispy and golden brown. Drain. Serve the lumpia with a side of the dipping sauce.

SPAM MUSUBI

HULA GIRL TRUCK—MIKALA BRENNAN—WASHINGTON, D.C.

MAKES 10 MUSUBI

Mikala Brennan insists you can't really run a Hawaiian food truck without having one particular, misunderstood food: Spam. "Spam is definitely one of those weird Hawaiian foods that is embedded in our culture," she says. "It's a weird anomaly on our menu, but we sell out every day." While the tinned meat can always be found in Continental grocery stores, it's rare to spot it on a menu. Not so in Hawaii: "Spam musubi is literally everywhere in Hawaii, including local convenience stores, grocery stores, school cafeterias and even at the zoo. Eating a Spam musubi seems to serve as a rite of passage for newcomers anxious to attain 'local' status."

SUSHI VINEGAR

1 cup (237ml) rice wine vinegar

½ cup (96g) sugar

1 tbsp (15g) kosher salt

MUSUBI

4 cups (842g) Calrose rice (sushi rice is a good substitute)

4 cups (946ml) water

1 tbsp (15g) furikake (found in Asian markets)

5 (7" x 8" [18 x 20cm]) sheets roasted nori (seaweed)

¼ cup (59ml) soy sauce

1 tsp sugar

1 (12-oz [340g]) can Spam

To make the sushi vinegar, heat the rice wine vinegar in a small saucepan over medium-low heat. Add the sugar and salt and stir until dissolved. Let cool and set aside. You can refrigerate for up to 2 weeks in an airtight container.

To make the musubi, steam the rice in the water according to package directions. Place in a bowl and let cool completely. Add 2 tablespoons (30ml) of the sushi vinegar and the furikake to the rice and mix thoroughly with your hands.

Cut the nori in half widthwise. This will give you 10 sheets.

Mix together the soy sauce and sugar and set aside.

Cut the Spam into 10 rectangular slices approximately ¼ inch (6mm) thick. In a large ungreased frying pan over medium heat (Spam has plenty of grease to keep it from sticking), fry the slices for 2 minutes, until brown and slightly crispy on both sides. Add the soy sauce and sugar mixture and let the Spam slightly braise for 1 to 2 minutes in the liquid. Set aside.

Using a Spam musubi press, place a piece of nori on a cutting board. Position the press on top of the nori so the length of the press is in the middle of the nori (widthwise). The press and the width of the nori should fit exactly the length of a slice of Spam. If you don't have a musubi press, you can open both sides of the empty Spam can, creating a musubi mold. On top of the nori, spread approximately ¼ cup (60g) of cooked rice across the bottom of the musubi press. Press the rice down with the flat part of the press to compact the rice. Place a slice of Spam on top of the rice (it should cover most of the length of the musubi press). Cover with an additional ¼ cup (60g) of rice. Remove the musubi from the press by pushing the whole stack down with the flat part of the press while lifting off the press. Fold one end of the nori over the musubi and press lightly onto the rice. Repeat with the other Spam slices.

Do not refrigerate musubi, as they will get dry and rubbery.

BOUDIN SAUSAGE POT STICKERS

NOLA GIRL FOOD TRUCK AND CATERING—DANNIELLE JUDIE—NEW ORLEANS, LA

MAKES 10 TO 12

While living in Atlanta, Dannielle Judie loved visiting the Asian farmers' markets. There she became quickly enamored with the pot stickers often served hot from the stalls. The hot, juicy dumplings seemed like the perfect vehicle for stuffing with just about anything. In this recipe, she re-creates them with New Orleans flair, replacing the standard pork with boudin sausage. "Basically, that's what New Orleans is," she says. "A hodgepodge of all cultures."

POT STICKERS

1 lb (454g) boudin sausage or pork-based sausage

10 napa cabbage leaves

1 tsp freshly grated ginger

3 scallions, thinly sliced

1 tsp chopped cilantro

1 tbsp (15ml) sesame oil

1 tbsp (15ml) soy sauce

½ tsp Tabasco or Sriracha sauce

1 to 2 tsp Creole seasoning, to taste

SESAME-GINGER SAUCE

¾ cup (180ml) soy sauce

1 tsp rice vinegar

1 tbsp (15ml) sesame oil

1 tbsp (15ml) orange juice

1 tbsp (15ml) water

½ tsp grated ginger

2 tbsp (25g) packed brown sugar

1 scallion, sliced

1 tsp cornstarch

7 tbsp (105ml) cold water

1 (10-oz [284g]) package gyoza or wonton wrappers

1 tbsp (15ml) sesame oil

Pinch of salt

To make the pot stickers, remove the skin from the sausage, break up the meat and place in a large bowl.

Cut the large white stem from the napa cabbage leaves and discard. Chop the remaining cabbage leaves and add to the meat mixture. Add the freshly grated ginger, sliced scallions, cilantro, sesame oil, soy sauce, Tabasco sauce and Creole seasoning. Mix all the ingredients well with a wooden spoon, cover and refrigerate for 30 minutes.

To make the sesame-ginger sauce, add all the ingredients to a small saucepan and bring to a simmer over medium heat for 10 minutes. Stir until the sugar has dissolved. Cool before serving.

In a small finger-sized bowl, add the cornstarch and 3 tablespoons (45ml) of the cold water. Mix until the cornstarch is dissolved.

On a clean surface, lay out 2 or 3 gyoza wrappers and scoop 1 tablespoon (15g) of filling in the middle of each wrapper. Brush the cornstarch water on all 4 sides of the wrapper and begin sealing the pot stickers. How you fold them is up to you. You can fold them into triangles by bringing two points together and sealing down the other two sides. Whichever way you decide to seal them, the key is to push the air out as you are sealing. Keep the wrappers moist under a towel and smooth any tears along the way.

In a large nonstick frying pan over medium heat, add the sesame oil and heat for 1 minute, or until the pan is hot. Add 6 to 8 pot stickers to the pan, being careful not to crowd them or let them touch. Allow the bottom of the pot stickers to cook for about 4 to 6 minutes, until brown but not burned.

Add the remaining ¼ cup (60ml) water to the pan, sprinkle a pinch of salt on the pot stickers and cover immediately. Allow the pot stickers to steam for about 5 to 6 minutes. Remove from the heat and serve immediately with the sesame-ginger sauce.

CHAPTER 8

GIVE ME MORE: SIDES

Sides are very much like the wisecracking sidekick. They're the complement to the entrée. The punch line that brings levity to a serious main dish. Who's Batman without Robin? What's a barbecued dinner without some baked beans? Sides never overpower the entrée. They are loyal and consistent, and you know that if you have a bad entrée, you can always look to a good ol' side to save the day. Heck, sometimes I just want to eat sides as my dinner. Are you one of those people who doesn't order fries with your burger? I don't know whether I can talk to you anymore then.

In this chapter you'll find a lot of building blocks to a complete meal. There are complementary sides like Homemade Kimchi from CJ's Street Food that can also be used atop different dishes. There are also sides that can be meals, like WhipOut!'s Fried Chicken Pups. Those frozen tots in your fridge will be a lot happier dressed like the G-Parm Tots from The Tot Cart. Or maybe you're just looking for a snack or something to bring to a potluck? There's a lot here to inspire you to take your meal to the next level.

BARONE MEATBALL COMPANY— STEPHEN DEWEY

RALEIGH/DURHAM, NORTH CAROLINA

In Italy, food and family are so intrinsically woven together, it's nearly impossible to imagine sitting down to a meal without being surrounded by at least two generations of relatives. To Stephen Dewey of the Barone Meatball Company, the smell of simmering marinara instantly transports him to a time when his mother and grandmother would spend all day preparing the family's evening meal. "The food I most looked forward to was their moist and flavorful meatballs," he recalls. "I always come back to those Barone family meatballs now."

Stephen has sixteen years of restaurant experience under his belt, from managing hamburger joints to taking on the role of sous chef at an upscale Italian restaurant. While his dream has always been to open up an Italian restaurant/sports bar of his own, a food truck seemed like a more realistic way to build up his clientele and introduce the masses to his stunning meatballs.

The wide variety of meatballs the Barone Meatball Company serves up on a rotating basis is a constant, pleasant surprise. "The key to a good meatball is making it juicy," says Stephen. "When you bite into them, they're almost like pillows, they're not dense and hard. You don't want to have to chew on it: it should almost melt in your mouth." With offerings such as the Black Bean and Corn Balls or the Crab Balls, Stephen breaks out of the standard ground-beef-and-marinara stereotype and creates dishes sure to please any palate.

Aside from introducing North Carolina to gourmet meatballs, Stephen wants to ensure that his customers get the same comforting, hearth-and-home feeling he remembers from his own childhood. "My goal is to make the customers feel like family, like they're regulars, like they're a part of it."

CRAB BALLS WITH REMOULADE

BARONE MEATBALL COMPANY—STEPHEN DEWEY—RALEIGH, NC

MAKES ABOUT 15 BALLS

Say good-bye to any preconceived notion you may have had about meatballs. Stephen Dewey uses fresh crab, scallions, Dijon mustard and Old Bay seasoning to create a delicate, flavorful meatball reminiscent of crab cakes. Enjoy them alone or on a hoagie roll topped with remoulade. When asked what he would like readers to get out of his recipes, Stephen says, "When people taste it, I want them to feel like, 'Wow, I can't believe I just made that.'"

REMOULADE

1 ¼ cups (275g) mayonnaise

¼ cup (63g) whole-grain Dijon mustard

1 tbsp (7g) paprika

1 ½ tsp (8g) Cajun seasoning

2 tsp (9g) horseradish

1 tsp lemon juice

1 tsp hot sauce

1 clove garlic, smashed and minced

CRAB BALLS

1 lb (453g) crabmeat

2 tbsp (28g) mayonnaise

1 tbsp (16g) Dijon mustard

1 egg

1 ½ tbsp (23g) Old Bay seasoning

2 tbsp (6g) chopped scallion

1 ½ cups (181g) Italian bread crumbs

1 cup (180g) grated Parmesan cheese

½ cup (65g) diced red and yellow bell pepper

Salt and pepper to taste

To make the remoulade, mix all the ingredients together in a bowl and adjust the seasoning to taste. Keep for a few hours in the refrigerator for best results.

Preheat the oven to 400°F (200°C, or gas mark 6). Grease a baking sheet.

To make the crab balls, mix all the ingredients together in a bowl. Form into 1-inch (2.5cm)-diameter balls and place on the greased pan. Bake for 10 minutes, then flip the crab balls and bake for an additional 10 minutes.

Serve with the remoulade.

TRADITIONAL SWABIAN SOFT PRETZELS

CAFÉ PROST—STEPHAN BAYER—RESEARCH TRIANGLE PARK, NC

MAKES 10 TO 12 SOFT PRETZELS

Stephan Bayer of Café Prost grew up eating these soft pretzels Germany. "At five o'clock my dad used to come home with a bag of fresh pretzels," reminisces Stephan. "That was a big part of my childhood. Ever since living stateside, I've wanted to just get a pretzel, but it was hard. So I decided to learn to make them." These pretzels are the real deal: crisp and caramelized on the outside, soft and fluffy on the inside. In keeping with European standards, the most accurate measurements are in grams.

DOUGH

11 cups (1100g) all-purpose flour

2 ½ cups (600ml) water

1 ½ tbsp (24g) salt

1 tbsp (14g) instant yeast

5 ½ tbsp (80g) unsalted butter, at room temperature

LYE BATH

¼ cup (40g) sodium hydroxide (food-grade), divided

34 oz (1000ml) water

Coarse sea salt or cheese, as desired, for topping

To make the dough, combine all the dough ingredients in a mixer fitted with the dough hook. On the lowest setting, mix the dough for 5 to 10 minutes, until it has an elastic consistency. There should be no lumps. Test the elastic consistency by picking up a section of dough with both hands and stretching it apart. Cover the bowl with a clean kitchen towel and let rest for 1 to 2 hours. If you have more time, try fermenting the dough by allowing it to rest for 5 to 8 hours overnight in the refrigerator. More rest yields more flavor.

Preheat the oven to 425°F (220°C, or gas mark 7). Line a baking sheet with parchment paper or a silicone mat.

To prepare and twist the pretzel, cut the dough into 3 ½-ounce (100g) pieces and begin rolling out into a long cylindrical shape 12 to 18 inches (30.5 to 45.5cm) long. Start rolling from the inside to the outside while putting more pressure on your two index fingers. The ends of the rolled-out dough should be thinner than the rest. These ends will be the pretzel arms. Twist the dough into a pretzel shape with a double knot. Place the pretzel on the baking sheet.

To make the lye bath, combine the sodium hydroxide and water in a container. Stir until the sodium hydroxide is fully dissolved. Be very careful with sodium hydroxide. It is caustic and will eat away at your skin. Use gloves and wear eye protection. If you want a safer method, baking soda may be used as a substitute but it will yield a different result.

With gloves on, carefully dip the twisted pretzel dough and submerge fully in the lye bath. Place the pretzel back onto the tray.

Add toppings as desired. For traditional pretzels, coat the pretzel with coarse sea salt. Other toppings include European cheeses such as Gouda or Emmental. Feel free to be creative.

Bake the pretzels until golden brown, about 8 to 10 minutes. Remove from the oven and let cool to room temperature before serving.

HOMEMADE KIMCHI

CJ'S STREET FOOD—MARK THOMAS—RALEIGH/DURHAM, NC

MAKES 1 ½ CUPS (240G)

This wonderful, fermented Korean cabbage is CJ's Street Food's most versatile condiment, so of course Mark ensures it's always made from scratch. They use it on everything; tacos, burritos, quesadillas, hot dogs, you name it. Mark taught himself the art of making kimchi and has enjoyed every moment researching the many different methods. To him, the perfect kimchi is all about balance: a little (but not too much) heat, a touch of sour and a bit of sweet funkiness. "I think the cool thing about kimchi is it can develop so many different layers of flavor. All the ingredients kind of blend together and do really crazy things on your palate when they have time to develop," he says. "The most important ingredient in it by far is TIME. It needs time to sit and do its thang!"

5 heads napa cabbage

2 to 4 tbsp (30 to 60g) salt

DRESSING

1 (25-oz [750ml]) bottle fish sauce

2 tbsp (31g) shrimp paste

1 tbsp (15ml) rice wine vinegar

½ cup (13g) red pepper flakes

2 tbsp (29g) minced ginger

1 tbsp (9g) minced garlic

1 cup (100g) roughly chopped scallion whites

2 cups (220g) shredded carrot

1 cup (110g) shredded daikon radish

Remove the hard ends of the cabbage heads, quarter lengthwise, and then cut across at ⅛- to ¼-inch (3 to 6mm) intervals. Place in a large container. Salt the cabbage evenly and generously. Mix loosely. Cover and refrigerate overnight. The next day, drain the liquid from the salted cabbage and discard the liquid.

To make the dressing, whisk the fish sauce, shrimp paste and rice wine vinegar in a bowl. Once evenly incorporated, whisk in the red pepper flakes, ginger, garlic and scallion. Taste the dressing. It should be hot and salty. If too fishy and salty, add a little water to dilute it slightly.

In an airtight container, combine the cabbage, dressing, carrots and daikon. Mix with a wooden spoon until everything is evenly coated with the dressing.

Cover and refrigerate. It needs time to sit. You can start enjoying it the next day, but it will achieve a deeper flavor if you can keep your hands out of it for 3 weeks.

POUTINE

RUA—JASON MYERS—PORTLAND, OR

SERVES 6

Jason Myers started off his career as a line cook, but found it was missing one key ingredient: the people. Opening up Rua allows him to be his own boss, source beautiful ingredients and, most importantly, interact with the customers lining up in front of his window. This is his take on the classic Canadian poutine, golden fries topped with cheese curds and rich gravy.

2 to 3 lb (907 to 1361g) potatoes (russet, Yukon gold or Kennebec)

GRAVY
4 cups (946ml) vegetable stock (unsalted or low sodium recommended)
½ cup (113g) unsalted butter
¾ cup (75g) all-purpose flour
1 ½ tsp (8ml) Worcestershire sauce
Kosher salt and black pepper to taste

2 to 3 qt (1.9 to 2.8l) rice bran oil or neutral-flavored oil
Kosher salt to taste
3 cups (360g) fresh cheese curds (cubed mozzarella works as a substitute)

Wash and peel the potatoes. Cut into ⅓- to ½-inch (8mm to 1.3cm) fries and submerge in water for 30 to 60 minutes. Drain the potatoes and rinse under cold water. Lay the fries out on paper towels and allow to dry.

To make the gravy, heat the vegetable stock in a saucepan over medium heat until it is just steaming. Melt the butter in a separate saucepan over medium heat and add the flour, stirring constantly. Add the stock and Worcestershire sauce to the butter and flour. The gravy will begin to thicken quickly. Reduce the heat to low and add salt and pepper to taste.

Pour the oil into a deep pot or fryer to a depth of 4 inches (10cm) and heat to 275°F (135°C) on a deep-fat thermometer. Working in small batches, cook the fries for 6 to 8 minutes, or until translucent. Remove from the oil and place on a cookie sheet covered with paper towels to absorb the excess oil. Repeat with the remaining potatoes, bringing the oil back to temperature between batches. Allow the potatoes to cool to room temperature.

Increase the heat of the oil to 375°F (190°C). Working again in small batches, cook the fries for about 5 minutes, or until golden brown. Remove from the oil and toss in a bowl lined with a paper towel. Add salt to taste.

Place the fries in a small bowl, add the cheese curds and cover generously with the hot gravy.

FRIED CHICKEN PUPS

WHIPOUT!—BRETT DOWNEY—EMERYVILLE, CA

SERVES 10

Owner Rob John of WhipOut! is a former teacher who became a little disillusioned with the state of education. Now he works with chef Brett Downey, cooking up high-end comfort food from a truck. Their fried chicken, smoked, brined, battered in their special mix, and then deep-fried is some of the best we've had. Here, Rob provides the recipe for the batter, herb lemon brine and even homemade ranch dressing for dipping.

HERB LEMON BRINE

1 cup (241g) kosher salt

2 qt (1.9l) water, plus 2 qt (1.9l) very cold water

10 sprigs thyme

1 bunch flat-leaf parsley

1 head garlic, cut in half horizontally

1 tbsp (8g) whole peppercorns

1 cup (341g) honey

6 lemons, halved

5 lb (2.3kg) boneless, skinless chicken thighs

1 lb (454g) apple wood chips

RANCH DRESSING

½ to ¾ cup (120 to 180ml) buttermilk

2 cups (502g) Garlic Aioli (see Crispy Meatloaf Sliders, page 52)

1 tbsp (15g) freshly ground black pepper

1 tbsp (15g) garlic powder

1 tbsp (15g) onion powder

Juice of 1 lemon

Kosher salt to taste

DRY BATTER

1 ½ lb (680g) all-purpose flour

¼ cup (60g) garlic powder

¼ cup (60g) onion powder

2 tbsp (30g) kosher salt

2 tbsp (15g) paprika

1 tsp cayenne

1 tsp freshly ground black pepper

Vegetable oil, for frying

1 qt (946ml) buttermilk

To make the brine, with the exception of the 2 quarts (1.9l) of very cold water, add all the brine ingredients to a large stockpot and bring to a boil over medium-high heat. Immediately remove from the heat. Let the brine cool for 15 to 20 minutes to allow the aromatics to steep and intensify the flavor. Add the 2 quarts (1.9l) of very cold water. When the brine is very cold (40°F [4.5°C] or lower), add the chicken and brine for 6 to 8 hours or overnight in the refrigerator.

Remove the chicken from the brine and lay in a flat even layer on a wire rack over a sheet tray. Allow to dry in the refrigerator for 1 hour. Drying the chicken will allow the smoke to penetrate the meat evenly.

In a barbecue grill, light a small amount of coals. Spread the coals evenly when they become red. Sprinkle the apple wood chips over the coals and place the cover on the grill. Check the grill for billowing smoke. The temperature should be a stable 300°F (149°C) and the chips should no longer be flaming. Place the chicken with the rack directly in the middle of the grill. Close the lid. Smoke the chicken for 45 minutes, until a meat thermometer inserted into the thickest thigh reads 165°F (74°C). Cool completely and cut each thigh into 5 or 6 even-size pieces.

To make the dressing, whisk the buttermilk into the aioli until creamy (you can use store-bought mayonnaise instead of aioli, just whisk in an additional ¼ cup [60ml] buttermilk). Whisk in the spices and lemon juice. Add salt to taste.

To make the batter, mix together all the dry batter ingredients in a bowl.

Pour the oil into a deep pot or fryer to 4 to 5 inches (10 to 13cm) and heat to 350°F (177°C) on a deep-fat thermometer. Working in small batches of 10 to 12 pieces, bread the chicken in the dry batter. Dip the breaded chicken into the buttermilk and let the excess drip off before breading the chicken in the dry batter for a second coating. Immediately drop the breaded chicken pups into the hot oil. Fry until crispy and golden brown for 5 minutes. Enjoy with the ranch dressing.

G-PARM TOTS

THE TOT CART—JULIE CRIST—PHILADELPHIA, PA

SERVES 4

Who says kids get to have all the fun? Next time you whip out a bag of tots for the little ones, give yourself a treat as well. Julie Crist take this already popular menu item to the next level with her creative, elaborate tot dishes. The G-Parm Tots, dusted with garlic and Parmesan cheese, are one of their most popular. "These tots are simple and delicious," says Julie, "although you may need a breath mint after eating them!"

---

1 (2 ½-lb [1134g]) bag frozen tots

4 tsp (20g) dried granulated garlic (not garlic powder)

4 tbsp (45g) grated Parmesan cheese

Prepare the tots according to the package instructions.

For each serving, place about 15 tots in a bowl. Sprinkle 1 teaspoon garlic and 1 tablespoon (11g) Parmesan cheese on top of the tots and swirl around the bowl a few times. Pour into a serving dish and enjoy!

COWBOY BEANS

FISHEY BIZNESS SEAFOOD CO.—DENNIS WHITE—AUSTIN, TX

SERVES 20 TO 25

In Texas, hospitality is the law of the land, especially when it comes to food. From the strings of lights decorating the eating area to charming red umbrellas and generous portions, the Fishey Bizness food truck goes to great lengths to radiate hospitality. Dennis White's food is equally comforting, especially the simple-yet-satisfying Cowboy Beans. "This recipe works well with seafood, barbecue or with anything else you can think of," Dennis says. "It's a real pot licker."

4 oz (113g) bacon

½ large onion, diced

2 fresh jalapeño peppers, seeded and diced

1 (3-lb [1.3kg]) can ranch-style beans

⅓ cup (84ml) Worcestershire sauce

⅓ cup (80ml) juice from pickled jalapeños

2 ¾ cups (553g) packed dark brown sugar

Chop the bacon into small pieces and place in a large pot over medium heat. Stir well for about 5 minutes. Add the onion and jalapeños and cook until the onions are soft for 5 to 6 minutes.

Add the beans, Worcestershire sauce, jalapeño juice and brown sugar and stir well. Reduce the heat to medium-low and cook for about 1 ½ hours, or until the beans are soft.

The amount of jalapeños and brown sugar may vary depending on taste. Some like it hot, some like it sweet. Season to taste.

KUBIDEH

CASPIAN KABOB—FIRUZEH DARCHINI (VICTOR'S MOM)—PORTLAND, OR

SERVES 4

"When I came to America, I asked my brother-in-law, 'What should I do for work?'" Victor Darchini recalls. "He said, 'Find something you love, because you're going to be doing it every day." So Victor found his true calling: grilling up savory, juicy, Persian-style street food to the Portland crowd. These skewers are made with ground lamb and beef and are perfect sprinkled with lime juice and sumac. "I enjoy feeding people," says Victor. "I love what I do."

---

1 lb (454g) twice-ground beef (top sirloin preferred)

1 lb (454g) twice-ground lamb shoulder

1 large yellow onion, finely grated and drained

½ tsp baking soda

2 tsp (10g) salt

1 tsp ground black pepper

Sumac to taste

Lime juice to taste

In a large bowl, add the beef, lamb, grated onion, baking soda, salt and pepper and mix. Knead the mixture for approximately 5 minutes until it feels sticky. Cover the bowl tightly with plastic wrap and place in the refrigerator for 2 hours.

Preheat a barbecue grill. Warm your hands with hot water and shape ⅓ pound (150g) of the meat around flat skewers. Place the skewers over (not on) the hot grill. Alternatively, you can form the meat into oblong meatballs and cook them on the hot grill.

After 2 to 3 minutes, flip the skewers and cook for an additional 2 to 3 minutes. The meat should be seared on the outside and juicy and tender on the inside. Sprinkle with sumac and lime juice to taste.

CURRY GARLIC PORTABELLA MUSHROOM FRIES WITH MUSTARD AIOLI

THE MORAL OMNIVORE—ROSS AND LINNEA LOGAS—MINNEAPOLIS, MN

SERVES 4 TO 6

"I secretly don't really like vegetables," Ross Logas of The Moral Omnivore in Minneapolis admits. Yet one look at their menu, and you can see vegetables are clearly the star of the show. "There are only so many meat sources in the world," says Ross's wife and partner-in-crime Linnea. "Vegetables I see as a whole other color palette." Ross was no stranger to fried portabella mushrooms, he'd made them often at the mom-and-pop pizzeria he'd managed for seven years. But to him, the usual tempura-battered mushrooms had one problem: they still tasted like mushrooms. He set about finding a way to fry and season a portabella in a way that would really wake up your taste buds. "It turns out that a portabella mushroom with curry, garlic and salt tastes amazing."

MUSTARD AIOLI

⅛ cup (30ml) cream

¼ tbsp (2g) flour

¼ cup (59ml) vegetable or chicken stock

2 tbsp (28g) mayonnaise

½ tbsp (8g) dijon mustard

1 tsp honey

¼ tsp chipotle powder

¼ tsp lemon juice

⅛ tsp chopped garlic

salt to taste

pinch of pepper

pinch of turmeric

4–6 large Portabella mushroom caps (24–30 slices)

2 cups (199g) flour

1 tbsp + ¾ tsp (18g) salt, divided

1 tbsp + ¾ tsp (9g) curry powder, divided

3 large eggs

2–3 cups (241–362g) panko bread crumbs

1 cup (237ml) canola oil

6 tbsp (60g) garlic, minced

To make the mustard aioli, heat the cream in a saucepan over medium heat for 2 to 3 minutes until the cream is hot. Slowly add the flour while constantly stirring the mixture. When it thickens and browns slightly, about 2 to 3 minutes, add the stock and continue to stir until the roux is fully incorporated with the stock. Remove from the heat. Add the mayonnaise, mustard, honey, chipotle powder, lemon juice, garlic, salt, pepper and tumeric. Mix together until it is fully incorporated. Set aside.

Next, remove any stems from the mushrooms. Using a small spoon, lightly scrape out the gills and wipe away any dirt from the outside with a dry cloth or soft brush. Slice the mushrooms into ¾-inch (1.9cm) slices.

Using three flat containers, combine the flour and 1 tablespoon (15g) of salt and 1 tablespoon (5g) of curry powder into the first container. Crack the eggs into the second container and whisk until smooth. In the third container, place the panko bread crumbs.

Moving in the same order, toss the mushrooms in flour and lightly shake to remove any excess flour. Dip in the whisked eggs until mushrooms are fully covered and then toss in the panko.

Heat the oil in a cast-iron skillet, or using a deep fryer set it to 375°F (191°C). Fry the mushrooms for 1 to 2 minutes or until the outside becomes golden brown. If necessary, turn over only once.

Working in 3 batches, toss 8 to 10 mushroom fries in a bowl with 2 tablespoons (20g) of garlic, and ¼ teaspoon of salt and curry powder. After removing the fries, scrape any garlic remaining in the bowl on top of the fries. Enjoy the mushrooms dipped in the mustard aioli.

CHAPTER 9

SIP, SIP, SIP: DRINKS

When we want to make a dish, we look up a recipe (from this book, obviously), go to the market, pick up fresh ingredients and spend time and effort to create something delicious to serve. But when we think of getting something to drink, too often than not we'll just grab a bottled drink with hard-to-pronounce chemical names.

There's a freshness that's expected in gourmet food carts. When you look into its belly, you often see fresh items sizzling on a hot grill and chefs feverishly chopping beautiful vegetables. Food cart owners put a lot of their soul into the food they put out, so it's refreshing (literally) to see another canvas for their creativity. Increasingly, we've seen chefs and owners adding homemade craft drinks to their menus to complete the experience for customers.

My day usually starts with a cup of coffee and ends with a gulp of water. Drinks are so automatic in our daily routine that it's nice to add a spin to them. We're frequently too content just buying drinks when we could be making our own delicious concoctions. Take coffee, for instance. Sure, it's so easy to just hit a button on the automatic coffeepot and let it percolate while you get ready for work. But learn how to make a hand-poured Chemex from HubBub Coffee Company in Philly and find out what artisanal truly tastes like. Or try a Turtle Power smoothie with kale, ginger and mango from Portland's own bike pedal–powered smoothie cart, Moberi. And end the day with a nice authentic Indian Chai from Parantha Alley in New York. Because, let's be honest, when you're eating one of their delicious paranthas, wouldn't one of their homemade teas pair a lot better than an orange soda?

MOBERI—RYAN CARPENTER
PORTLAND, OREGON

What happens when a vintage Schwinn exercise bicycle meets a blender? If it's Ryan Carpenter doing the pedaling, the result is fresh fruit and veggie smoothies packed with nutrients. The Moberi food cart, home of the bicycle-powered blender, has to be one of the most unique—and fun—food carts we've seen.

Ryan came up with the idea when a fellow traveler at an Australian hostel showed him a YouTube video of a Guatemalan village. The villagers had taken old bicycles at the end of their life cycle (no pun intended) and turned them into "bicimaquinas," useful, efficient machines used for everything from pumping water to shelling macadamia nuts. The video clip got Ryan's wheels turning, and by spring 2011 he was back in Portland working on a bicimaquina of his own.

Moberi has since grown from that first setup of bicycle, blender and homemade sink to a full-on kitchen on wheels. "It's neat being a part of the food cart community," he says. "It's more burgeoning and has that unique edge to it that restaurants will never have. If it's served out of a trailer, you've got a certain amount of intrigue right away." Having the option of hopping on a bicycle to blend your own smoothie certainly doesn't hurt. No matter how they're blended, Ryan's smoothies are a tasty way to deliver health-boosting vitamins and antioxidants. (The pedaling is optional.)

ONE NIGHT IN BANGKOK

MOBERI—RYAN CARPENTER AND LINDSEY HAMILTON—PORTLAND, OR

SERVES 1

Ryan Carpenter saw his One Night in Bangkok smoothie as a challenge. He was curious to see whether he could incorporate the spicy chile flavor of Sriracha into a great-tasting smoothie. Peanut butter and banana ended up being the perfect companions to the popular hot sauce. "It was a point of pride to put it on the menu," Ryan says.

---

8 oz (220ml) milk or almond milk

2 tbsp (16g) vanilla whey protein

1 to 2 tbsp (11 to 22g) peanut butter

1 tbsp (16ml) Sriracha

3 oz (85g) frozen banana

3 oz (85g) ice

Load the blender in order of softness: liquids first to frozen ingredients last. In this order add the milk, vanilla whey protein, peanut butter, Sriracha, frozen banana and ice. Once all the ingredients are loaded, blend until smooth.

TURTLE POWER

MOBERI—RYAN CARPENTER—PORTLAND, OR

SERVES 1

Turtle Power has to be one of the tastiest ways to get your greens. The sweetness of mango and banana and the bite of ginger highlight and elevate the earthy kale and spinach. You may even get Leonardo, Michelangelo, Donatello and Raphael to put down their pizzas for this one.

---

8 oz (227ml) apple juice

½ cup (170g) chopped kale, no stems

½ cup (170g) spinach

½ banana

1 tbsp (14g) grated ginger

3 oz (85g) frozen mango

3 oz (85g) ice

1 orange slice, for garnish

Load the blender in order of softness: liquids first to frozen ingredients last. In this order add the apple juice, kale, spinach, banana, ginger, frozen mango and ice. Once all the ingredients are loaded, blend until smooth. Garnish with an orange slice.

CHEMEX BREWED COFFEE

HUBBUB COFFEE COMPANY—DREW CROCKETT—PHILADELPHIA, PA

SERVES 1

It took a trip to Sydney, Australia, of all places for Drew Crockett of HubBub Coffee to fully fall in love with coffee culture. But it wasn't just the focus on specialty coffee that he loved; he was smitten with the use of the hot beverage as a medium for social interaction. "On a very simplistic level, coffee is a way for us to interact with friends and people we've yet to meet," Drew explains. "A lot of people feel intimidated when they walk into certain coffee shops; our goal is to break down that barrier. It's our obligation as coffee people to open up to customers and engage them." Think of this Chemex single-serving recipe as a handshake. You'll need a Chemex coffeemaker and Chemex bonded paper filter for this, along with a scale for accurate measuring.

1 oz (28g) whole bean coffee
(we use Stumptown Coffee)

15 oz (425ml) water

Place the paper filter in the Chemex coffeemaker (three-folded side near the spout) and rinse the filter thoroughly so that the entire filter is saturated. Empty the water into the sink.

Grind your coffee to a size similar to kosher salt.

Boil the water in a kettle. Let cool to 200°F (93°C).

Add the coffee to the paper filter. Place the Chemex with the coffee on a scale.

Set a kitchen timer for 3 minutes. Start the timer and make the first pour by wetting all of the grounds with the boiling water. Slowly pour 3 ½ ounces (100ml) of water. Pour as evenly as possible to ensure a consistent extraction.

At 2 minutes remaining, slowly make your second pour of 7 ounces (200ml) of water.

At 1 minute remaining, pour 4 ½ ounces (125ml) of water.

Serve in a warmed coffee mug.

INDIAN CHAI

PARANTHA ALLEY—RAJEEV YERNENI AND RETU SINGLA—NEW YORK, NY

SERVES 8

Chai tea is arguably one of the most popular Indian exports to make its way into daily American life. Traditionally, this drink is a black tea mixed with various aromatic Indian spices and served with or without milk. Chai tea recipes can be as much a creative and reflective expression as a signature. The recipe below is Rajeev Yerneni's personal concoction served at the Parantha Alley food stand. Enjoy this fragrant brew on its own or sweet and milky.

4 cups (907ml) water

8 black tea bags

½ tsp ground cinnamon or
½ cinnamon stick

½ tsp ground cardamom or
3 or 4 whole pods, cracked open

½ tsp ground cloves or
3 or 4 whole cloves

½" (1.3cm) piece ginger, grated

3 or 4 black peppercorns

Sugar to taste

4 cups (907ml) milk

Heat the water in a pot over medium-high heat to the verge of boiling. Reduce the heat to medium-low and add the tea bags, cinnamon, cardamom, cloves, ginger, black peppercorns and sugar to taste. Steep for approximately 3 minutes, adjusting the heat to keep the water on the verge of boiling. Add the milk and stir occasionally. Bring the chai to a boil over medium-high heat. Boil until the chai has reached the desired consistency. Add more sugar to taste and serve.

CHAPTER 10

SWEET TOOTH: DESSERTS

I'm an odd person. For a while, I never really understood why people ordered dessert after a meal. Not that I didn't love eating sweets or wasn't in awe of the craft of making desserts. I loved a cupcake or a doughnut here and there, but desserts didn't make me drool like so many people I know. It was my obsession with specialty coffee the past couple of years that really helped me understand the importance of desserts. Of course, I started drinking my coffee with lots of milk and sugar (I hate my old self for that) and progressed into drinking it all black, the way it was meant to be appreciated.

With every cup of coffee I drank, I felt like I needed something afterward. Like my palate was yearning for something that I couldn't explain. So I started drinking my cup of coffee and pairing it with cookies or pastries. It's like in that scene in *Ratatouille* where Remy is explaining to his brother about how the right combination of food can create fireworks in your head. Something clicked, and that was just the beginning.

I caved and started ordering desserts at restaurants. I finally started understanding the balance it brings to your meal. I now can't imagine eating a meal without dessert as the finale. It's like sitting through a movie and leaving before the ending. We hope these desserts, like the beignets from Rua in Portland or the Daifuku Mochi from Poi Dog Philly, complete your meal and leave you with your taste buds tingling. And if you want to eat dessert as your whole meal, no judgments here.

THE TREATS TRUCK—KIM IMA

NEW YORK, NEW YORK

For Kim Ima, the joy of baking doesn't end with a finished product. It's only the beginning. "I love the anticipation of sharing," she says of her assortments of brownies, cookies and baked goodies. "The treat is more than the actual thing you've made, but the giving of it to yourself or to a friend." Kim has a long history of baking for others. As a performer at the La MaMa Experimental Theatre Club in New York, she would often come to rehearsals bearing freshly baked treats, which quickly became in demand with the rest of the company.

With her teammates' encouragement and her lifetime love of baking, starting up a food truck seemed like a no-brainer. "I could see it all of a sudden one day: the Treats Truck," she recalls. "It was like instant love." Kim dove in. With no official culinary training or experience as a professional baker, she found herself at the helm of a commercial kitchen. "It didn't occur to me to be intimidated," she says. "When you really want to try something, it's probably good you don't have the whole picture. The unknown is one of those ingredients for opening yourself up to what you can do."

The Treats Truck has been spreading happiness through baked goods since 2007. Kim's secret is getting to know her customers, learning what they love and letting them inspire her. "You can trace the evolution of a lot of the treats to one person." It's not unusual for her customers' names to show up on her menu along with the pastry they've helped spark. Kim's love of sharing has found the perfect outlet in her rolling bakery where her primary goal is to give people a chance to pause and relax in their fast-paced lives. "The Treats Truck is a place you can come and get things with sprinkles and glitter sugar. A little treat in the middle of an ordinary day. The bottom line is: it's about making you smile."

VANILLA OR CINNAMON DOUGHNUTS

THE TREATS TRUCK—KIM IMA—NEW YORK, NY

MAKES ABOUT 18 DOUGHNUTS

Kim loves doughnuts, but the lack of a deep fryer on The Treats Truck presented a dilemma. Her solution? Bake 'em! "It ended up being a delightful discovery," she says. "It's so simple." She recommends using doughnut pans. They're similar to a muffin pan, easy to use and available at most kitchen stores.

DOUGHNUT BATTER

6 oz (191ml) vegetable oil

1 ⅛ cups (216g) sugar

3 eggs

2 ¼ tsp (16g) vanilla extract

2 ¼ cups (224g) flour

2 ¼ tsp (8g) baking powder

⅜ tsp salt

¾ cup (183ml) milk

Melted butter, for dipping

Sugar or cinnamon sugar, for dipping

To make the batter, mix the oil and sugar together in a bowl with an electric mixer. Next add the eggs and vanilla and beat again.

In a separate bowl, mix the flour, baking powder and salt. Slowly add the dry mixture to the mixer. Add the milk and beat again, just until incorporated. Be careful not to overmix. Use right away or refrigerate until you are ready to bake. Make the batter the night before for a speedy breakfast treat.

Preheat the oven to 350°F (180°C, or gas mark 4). Grease the doughnut pan with a bit of oil or cooking spray. Use a piping bag to pipe in the batter. A sandwich baggie with a corner cut for the tip can be used in lieu of a piping bag. The batter rises, so fill the mold halfway. Bake for 10 to 15 minutes, until the doughnuts are baked through, but are still moist and soft. Cool in the pan.

Put the melted butter in a shallow bowl. Put some sugar in another shallow bowl. Dip each doughnut into the butter on both sides. Then dip the doughnut in the sugar on both sides. Repeat with each doughnut. Then, pour yourself a cup of coffee or a glass of milk and dig in!

CHOCOLATE PRETZEL CRISPY SQUARES

THE TREATS TRUCK—KIM IMA—NEW YORK, NY

MAKES 9 TO 12 SQUARES

"If you've grown up in the U.S., chances are you've made Rice Krispies treats. They're just so pleasurable. Even at the fanciest weddings, you put out a Rice Krispies treat, and people are happy." Kim's lifelong love of Rice Krispies treats ensures that some variation of them is always available on her truck. This particular recipe uses chocolate and pretzels to hit that sweet and salty spot.

---

3 tbsp (43g) butter, plus more for pan

10 oz (284g) marshmallows (mini or big)

6 ½ cups (138g) rice cereal

¾ cup (121g) pretzel bits (smash or break apart small salted pretzels)

½ cup (90g) semisweet chocolate chips

¼ to ½ cup (45 to 90g) white chocolate chips

Grease a 9 x 13-inch (23 x 33cm) baking pan with a pat of butter.

Melt the butter in a large pot over low heat. As the butter melts, add the marshmallows. Stir until everything is melted and remove the mixture from the heat as soon as the marshmallows have melted.

Pour in the cereal and stir. Stir in the pretzels followed by the chocolate chips and white chocolate chips. Pour the mixture into the greased baking pan.

Let stand for 10 to 15 minutes before you cut into squares.

BEIGNETS

RUA—JASON MYERS—PORTLAND, OR

MAKES APPROXIMATELY 25 BEIGNETS

Jason Myers has had many careers in his life, but cooking and interacting with customers are the things that have brought him the most joy. He started Rua as a way to cook while still being close to the people. And what better way to keep the people coming than with hot, made-to-order beignets. Brought to Louisiana by eighteenth-century French colonists, these pastries are rarely seen as far as Portland, Oregon. So thank heavens for Jason, or we'd never get our hands on his fried, sugar-dusted, classic beignets.

1 ½ tsp (5g) active dry yeast

¾ cup (177ml) lukewarm water

¼ cup (50g) packed light brown sugar

1 tsp kosher salt

½ tsp vanilla extract

½ cup (122g) evaporated milk

2 tbsp (28g) vegetable shortening

1 egg, lightly beaten to break yolk

3 ¼ cups (323g) all-purpose flour, plus more for kneading

Vegetable oil, for frying

½ cup (65g) powdered sugar

Add the yeast and water to a stand mixer. Turn the mixer on low. Add the brown sugar, salt and vanilla. Continue to mix for about 2 minutes. Add the evaporated milk, shortening and egg. Continue mixing on low for another 2 minutes.

Add half of the flour and mix on low for 1 minute. Add the remaining flour and mix for 4 more minutes. Make sure that all of the liquid has been incorporated into the flour. The mixture may still be lumpy but do not overwork the dough or you'll get a tough beignet.

Scrape the dough into a large bowl using a rubber spatula. Cover with plastic wrap and chill for at least 8 hours.

Place the dough on a heavily floured surface about 2 ½ by 2 ½ feet (76 by 76cm). Liberally dust the surface of the dough with flour until it is no longer sticky. Using a rolling pin, roll out the dough gently, flouring any sticky spots, until it is slightly thicker than ⅛ inch (3mm).

Pour the oil into a deep pot or fryer to a depth of 3 inches (7.5cm) and heat to 375°F (191°C) on a deep-fat thermometer.

Using a pastry wheel or a pizza cutter, cut the dough into 2 by 2-inch (5 by 5cm) squares. The squares will probably contract a bit and end up being more of a rectangular shape. In small batches of 5 at a time, place the beignets in the hot oil. They will sink to the bottom before rising to the top. Once they surface, use metal tongs to flip them over a few times in the oil until they start to puff up. Once puffed, let the beignets sit in the oil until one side is golden brown and then flip to brown the other side.

Remove the beignets from the oil and allow to cool slightly. Place 5 beignets in a small paper bag, add 1 tablespoon (8g) of powdered sugar and shake to coat. Enjoy immediately.

BUTTER MOCHI CAKE WITH SALTED COCONUT CREAM

CARTE BLANCHE—JESSIE ARON—PORTLAND, OR

MAKES 18 SQUARES

Don't try to pin Jessie Aron down on her style of food. "People are always asking us what kind of food we serve," she laughs. "And it's hilarious and sad that I don't have an answer to the most basic question ever. We do have multiethnic influences, but I wouldn't consider it fusion. It's edible jazz." You can see this in her Butter Mochi Cake. Inspired by the Hawaiian mochi cake, it includes a Thai coconut cream and is finished off with fresh Pacific Northwest berries.

CAKE

3 cups (454g) Mochiko rice flour

2 ½ cups (479g) sugar

2 tsp (8g) baking powder

½ tsp salt

2 cups (473ml) coconut milk or coconut cream, preferably the Aroy-D brand

5 large eggs

½ cup (115g) salted butter, melted

½ tsp almond extract

½ tsp vanilla extract

SALTY SWEET COCONUT CREAM

2 cups (473ml) coconut milk or coconut cream

2 tbsp (24g) sugar, plus more to taste

1 ½ tsp (8g) salt

1 pandan leaf, fresh or frozen and tied in a knot to release aroma (optional)

1 to 2 cups (180 to 360g) of your favorite fresh berries (if berries aren't in season, any stone fruit will do)

Preheat the oven to 350°F (180°C, or gas mark 4) and grease a 13 by 9-inch (33 by 23cm) pan.

To make the cake, whisk together the rice flour, sugar, baking powder and salt in a large bowl.

In another bowl, whisk together the coconut milk, eggs, melted butter, almond extract and vanilla extract. Add the wet mixture to the dry mixture, whisking or beating with an electric hand mixer on low until the batter is fully incorporated.

Pour the batter into the baking pan and smooth the top. Bake for about 1 ½ hours, until golden brown and the cake begins to pull away from the sides of the pan. Check after 1 hour for doneness. Allow the cake to cool on a rack. Cut the cake into squares.

To make the coconut cream, combine the coconut milk, sugar, salt and pandan leaf in a small saucepan and bring to a simmer over medium-low heat. Be careful to not boil over the coconut milk. Simmer for 15 to 20 minutes, uncovered, until it coats the back of a spoon. Remove the pandan leaf. Taste the sauce and adjust the levels of salt and sugar to your liking. The taste should be similar to a thin salted caramel sauce. Set aside and let cool.

Add 1 tablespoon (15ml) of the salty sweet coconut cream in the center of a plate. Position a square of mochi cake on top of the sauce and generously ladle more salty sweet coconut cream over the top of the cake. Finish with fresh berries.

TRES LECHES CAKE WITH COFFEE SAUCE

TACO MONDO—MICHAEL SULTAN AND CAROLYN NGUYEN—PHILADELPHIA, PA

SERVES 8 TO 10

Tres Leches Cake is a delightfully buttery cake soaked in three types of milk. Michael Sultan was all set to make a Vietnamese coffee tres leches cake when he realized one thing: he had forgotten the Vietnamese coffee mixture. Luckily, he's on good terms with the guys at Rival Bros Coffee. One quick phone call and a homemade coffee syrup was on its way. It's been such a hit, it's even turned the heads of a few food critics. If you can't get your hands on Rival Bros in your area, feel free to use any high-quality espresso.

COFFEE SAUCE

¼ cup (50g) packed light brown sugar

1 cup (235ml) hot high-quality espresso (we use Rival Bros)

¼ cup (59ml) whole milk

¼ cup (88g) sweetened condensed milk

¼ cup (59ml) half-and-half

CAKE

3 ½ cups (315g) cake flour

2 cups (383g) sugar

1 tbsp (11g) baking powder

½ tsp salt

1 cup (225g) unsalted butter, at room temperature

1 cup (237ml) whole milk

1 cup (237ml) vegetable oil

4 large eggs

2 large egg whites

1 tbsp (8g) lime zest

To make the coffee sauce, dissolve the brown sugar in the hot espresso. Add the whole milk, condensed milk and half-and-half. Refrigerate the sauce until ready to use.

Preheat the oven to 350°F (180°C, or gas mark 4). Line a 12 by 18-inch (30.5 by 46cm) sheet pan with parchment paper and lightly coat with cooking spray.

To make the cake, sift the flour, sugar, baking powder and salt into a mixer with a whisk attachment. On medium speed, add butter and milk and blend for about 4 minutes, until smooth. Add the oil and blend until incorporated.

In a separate bowl, combine the eggs, egg whites and lime zest and mix well. Add all at once to the flour and butter mixture and mix thoroughly. Pour into the pan and bake for 12 to 15 minutes, or until a toothpick inserted into the center comes out clean.

Let cool slightly, then cut into squares and spoon the sauce on top.

DAIFUKU MOCHI

POI DOG PHILLY—KIKI ARANITA AND CHRIS VACCA—PHILADELPHIA, PA

MAKES ABOUT 25 PIECES

After growing up in Hawaii and China, Kiki Aranita went to college in Italy. But of all the places she's been, Hawaii is home to the flavors she misses most. She honors her Chinese and Hawaiian heritage by offering two kinds of mochi: butter mochi and daifuku mochi. Butter mochi is similar to a dense, soft cake and is sliced into squares from a pan. Daifuku mochi is also made from rice flour, but it's rounded and stuffed with a variety of fillings. Kiki suggests cookie butter or fruit preserves for a truly satisfying treat.

---

1 cup (192g) sugar

2 cups (473ml) hot water

2 cups (303g) Mochiko rice flour

A few drops food coloring (optional)

Katakuriko (potato starch), for dusting

6 to 7 tbsp (120 to 140g) filling of your choice (fruit preserves, cookie butter, etc.)

Set a saucepan over low heat and dissolve the sugar in the hot water. Whisk in the Mochiko flour until smooth. To color the mochi, add a few drops of your food coloring of choice.

Pour the mixture into a bamboo steamer lined with parchment paper. Split the mixture into 2 steamers if needed. Steam for 20 minutes; it should look like an elastic dough.

Dust a baking sheet with the katakuriko. Flip the parchment paper mochi-side down onto the dusted baking sheet. While hot, carefully peel off the parchment with a spatula. Let cool for no longer than 1 minute or it will begin to set.

Dust your hands with katakuriko before handling the mochi. Pull off sections that weigh about 1 ¼ ounces (35g) and press between your palms into round disks about ½ inch (1.3cm) thick. Place ¾ teaspoon of your desired filling in the center and pinch the sides of the disk around and together so that the filling is contained.

Put the mochi pinched-side down in a mini paper muffin cup and then immediately into a mini muffin tin so the mochi retains its shape.

Serve immediately or wrap the entire tin tightly in plastic wrap. Do not refrigerate.

SALTED CARAMEL BANANA CREAM PIE

RUE CHOW—JARETT AND RACHEL EYMARD—NEW ORLEANS, LA

MAKES 1 PIE

Rachel Eymard of Rue Chow loves the creativity of putting her own modern spin on the classics. She updates banana cream pie with a salted caramel sauce and rich caramel whipped cream. Sprinkle it all with a bit of sea salt, and you've got a decadent dessert you'll want to take your time to enjoy.

CARAMEL SAUCE
⅓ cup (79ml) water
1 ½ cups (288g) sugar
1 cup (244ml) heavy cream
1 tbsp (14g) butter
2 tsp (10g) salt
1 tsp (7g) vanilla extract

FILLING
¾ cup (183ml) milk
¼ cup (48g) sugar
3 egg yolks, at room temperature
2 tbsp (19g) cornstarch
1 ½ tsp (7g) butter
Pinch of salt
½ tsp vanilla extract
1 (14-oz [392g]) can condensed milk
1 cup (243ml) heavy cream, whipped to stiff peaks

SALTED CARAMEL WHIPPED CREAM
2 ½ cups (609ml) heavy cream
⅔ Caramel Sauce (see recipe above)

1 graham cracker crust
2 bananas
Finishing salt

To make the caramel sauce, combine the water and sugar in a saucepan. Do not stir. Turn the heat to medium-high and cook until the sugar is completely dissolved and turns a nutty brown. Add the cream, butter, salt and vanilla and stir. Cool to room temperature and set aside.

For the pie filling, warm the milk, sugar and yolks in a heavy-bottomed saucepan over medium heat, stirring continuously. Add the cornstarch and whisk until thick. Remove from the heat, put through a fine-mesh sieve into a bowl and then stir in the butter, salt and vanilla. Press plastic wrap directly onto the filling and chill in the refrigerator.

To make the whipped cream, mix the cream and the caramel sauce in a bowl and whip to stiff peaks. Reserve enough caramel sauce to drizzle on top of the finished pie.

Remove the chilled filling from the refrigerator, stir in the condensed milk, then fold in the whipped cream. Return to the refrigerator and chill for 1 more hour.

Spoon some of the filling into the graham cracker crust and spread evenly with the back of a spoon. Cut the bananas into rounds and layer some slices over the filling. Layer more filling, and then more bananas, until all of the filling and bananas are used. Top the pie with the salted caramel whipped cream and drizzle the remaining caramel sauce over the pie. Sprinkle with a touch of salt and enjoy.

CHAPTER 11

LICK IT: POPS

Is this a whole chapter dedicated to just pops? You're damn right it is. We noticed an interesting trend when we started putting this book together. We found carts from different parts of America selling one specific item: ice pops. Don't use the term *Popsicle*, though (it's trademarked). But these ice pops aren't the ones you find on the ice cream truck, with colors you choose because that's the color you want your tongue to be. These are handmade with fresh, seasonal ingredients. They display creativity and beauty to match any other dessert you can think of.

If you have kids in the house, these are great snacks that store well and are super easy to make. Just pick up a mold and make a Kiwi Mango pop from Fat Face (my vote for one of the best cart names ever) in San Francisco or, for yourself, a Vietnamese Iced Coffee pop from Lil' Pop Shop in Philly. Bottom line: you know what goes into that pop, and it's not green and orange food coloring.

Here's a couple of tips from the pros. The less time it takes to freeze in the freezer, the better the texture will be. And turn the freezer to the coldest setting for faster freezing or use a home quick-freeze pop maker. So what are you waiting for?

MELTDOWN—MICHELLE WEAVER
NEW ORLEANS, LOUISIANA

The siren song of the ice cream truck. Anyone who's been a child during a hot summer day remembers the immediate Pied Piper reaction to the jingling melody playing from an ice cream truck. Standing on the sidewalk, clutching a dollar bill, eyeing the pictures of Push Pops, Fudgsicles and Drumsticks plastered on the vehicle's side is a childhood memory shared by most Americans. Michelle Weaver of Meltdown doesn't think kids should have a monopoly on the experience. "Everything an ice pop represents is happy and fun and exciting," she says. "That's what I want to convey." The distinctly grown-up flavors of her handmade gourmet pops convey it quite well. Standing in front of her truck, clutching your dollar in your hand, eyeing the combinations of fruits and herbs, makes you feel as giddy as a kid again.

Michelle started out in sunny Los Angeles, where *paletas*, the Mexican version of ice pops, became her refreshment of choice. "I was just kind of obsessed with them and the fact that you have so many fruits readily available in California all year. I just started putting my own twist on the Mexican *paleta* and doing a lot of herbaceous combinations with fruits." She purchased a 1971 postal-vehicle-turned-ice-cream-truck and converted its scary clown motif (think John Wayne Gacy) into a modern retro look cute enough to fit in at catered events. While she carried all the usual ice cream and fruit pops found on any standard ice cream truck, it wasn't until she relocated to New Orleans that she had the courage to start selling her own creations. They were a hit. "Every time we stopped, no one wanted the prepackaged stuff. They wanted my homemade artisanal pops."

CHAPTER 12

PUNCH IT UP: SAUCES

When I lived in Japan, I frequently heard the same story about how important a sauce is to a chef. If a sushi restaurant is burning down, the first thing they would run back in to grab is their soy sauce. How often have we heard that term *special sauce* or *secret sauce*? Or as the Epic Meal Time crew on YouTube likes to say, "Sauuuuce!" We've seen many a food cart become famous for their sauce alone.

Are you the type of person who orders fries and eats them straight? Or are you the type of person who gets a million different sauces to dip your fries in? If you're the latter, I'd like to be your friend. I'm obsessed with sauces. You will never catch me eating fried chicken without dipping it in a big vat of gravy. The right dressing can really change a dish. An undressed person sounds appealing, but an undressed chicken, not so much.

If you're feeling like your dish is missing something, this is the chapter to read. Sauces can work in both directions: as a topping or as a foundation to build upon. For example, you could use CJ's Street Food's Thai-Style Vinaigrette as a salad dressing or as a marinade for meat. What you might have found ho-hum before was probably just missing a sauce. Heck, sometimes I just want to drink a sauce as my dinner.

MAYHEM AND STOUT—
STEVE APPLEGATE AND JAY BROWN

NEW YORK, NEW YORK

Jay Brown of Mayhem and Stout seems to have a habit of putting his money where his mouth is. Putting his art history graduate degree to good use, he spent some time working at an advertising agency before coming to the realization that he hated every second of it. "Basically, one day I was on the phone with my girlfriend (now my wife) and she said, 'Well, why don't you just quit?'" he recalls. "I just happened to be feeling ballsy that day, so I quit." A free man, Jay returned to his first love: cooking. After reaching the ranks of executive chef and sous chef, Jay had another saucy idea while drinking with a childhood friend at a Christmas party. "We were drunk enough that we decided we were going to start a sandwich shop. It was a little insane."

Mayhem and Stout doesn't serve your average sandwiches. Jay took his cue from his sous chef experience at a previous fine dining establishment, in which a brunch menu featuring leftover braised meats from the previous evening's less successful dinners were a huge hit. Jay's sandwiches feature similar flavorful, tender braised meats but with the addition of creative, inspired sauces to provide an ever-changing, mix-and-match experience.

It's hard to say whether Mayhem and Stout's sauces or meats command more attention. Jay has a knack for inventive combinations that bring out the best in his ingredients. He credits his love of foodie publications for his innovative ideas. "I read everything that can possibly be written about food. I'll flip through *Good Housekeeping* or *Saveur* or a James Beard–awarded cookbook. I have 300-some-odd cookbooks. Even when I think I know everything that's in those cookbooks, I'll go back and get inspiration." This is one cookbook we're hoping he'll add to his collection.

BUTTERNUT SQUASH MUSTARD

MAYHEM AND STOUT—JAY BROWN—NEW YORK, NY

MAKES 1 QUART (700G)

"I hate eating something that doesn't punch me in the face a little bit," says Jay Brown. "Why bother? We try to shake people up a little bit with flavor." This sweet, rich, zesty mustard has flavor in spades. It goes well with just about anything, but Jay notes it goes particularly well with any type of pork dish, especially bacon.

1 large butternut squash, halved and seeded, but not peeled

Olive oil, for rubbing

Salt and pepper to taste

2 cups (450g) whole-grain mustard

2 tbsp (40g) honey

Preheat the oven to 350°F (180°C, or gas mark 4). Rub the squash on all sides with oil and sprinkle lightly with salt and pepper. Put the squash on a baking sheet and roast for 30 to 45 minutes, until beautifully golden and bubbly and a knife slides through with almost zero effort. Remove the squash from the oven and scoop out all the roasted pulp from the skin.

Stay away from spicy brown or yellow mustard, which drowns out anything you add to it. Add the whole-grain mustard and squash pulp to a food processor or blender with a standard blade and pulse until incorporated. Once combined, add the honey and salt and pepper to taste and puree for less than 1 minute, until there are no lumps from the squash.

Serve with any meat or put on almost any sandwich.

ROASTED CITRUS VINAIGRETTE

MAYHEM AND STOUT—JAY BROWN—NEW YORK, NY

MAKES 1 QUART (750ML)

The delicate, bright, acidic flavors of this vinaigrette pair perfectly with lighter meats, such as chicken and pork. Jay recommends it especially as a salad dressing or as a marinade for shrimp or white fish. "Don't be afraid to roast the hell out of the citrus," he advises. "Put it on any greens, meats or fish. Or s*#t, brush your teeth with it, because it's awesome!"

2 oranges (we use Cara Cara oranges or Florida juicing oranges)

2 lemons

2 limes

1 grapefruit

1 ½ cups (354ml) olive oil, plus more for rubbing

Salt to taste

2 tbsp (31g) whole-grain mustard

1 tbsp (13g) packed dark brown sugar

Preheat the oven to 400°F (200°C, or gas mark 6). Cut all the fruit in half. Rub the fruit lightly with olive oil and lightly season with salt. Put the fruit cut-side down on a baking sheet and roast for 15 to 20 minutes, or until the cut sides of the fruit begin to brown. Remove from the oven and let cool slightly.

Squeeze every ounce of flesh and juice out of the fruit into a strainer. Strain the juice into a blender. Pick out any seeds from the strainer and add the remaining pulp to the juice. Add the mustard and brown sugar and blend for 15 to 30 seconds.

With the blender running, slowly drizzle in the olive oil until the mixture fully emulsifies and you have a thick dressing.

HOMEMADE BASIL PESTO

FRENCHEEZE FOOD TRUCK—JASON ROBINSON KING—NEW ORLEANS, LA

MAKES 2 CUPS (450G)

"Before I started Frencheeze," says Jason King of his New Orleans–based truck, "I was lying around on my couch, complaining about my life and being angry." A former attorney who had recently realized his legal career was taking too much of a toll, Jason found himself at a crossroads. It took his wife's tough love and encouragement to give him the push he needed to start up a food truck serving gourmet grilled cheese sandwiches with toppings such as this delicious basil pesto.

½ cup (63g) pine nuts

4 cups (161g) fresh basil leaves

1 cup (120g) grated Parmesan cheese

3 cloves garlic, roughly chopped

Zest and juice or 1 lemon

¾ tsp kosher salt

¼ tsp coarse black pepper

1 cup (235ml) extra-virgin olive oil

Toast the pine nuts in a skillet for 5 to 6 minutes over medium heat until lightly golden in color and fragrant. Remove from the pan and let cool.

In a food processor, add the basil, Parmesan cheese, pine nuts, garlic, lemon zest and juice, salt and pepper. Slowly drizzle in the olive oil while mixing.

To freeze the pesto for later use, spoon 2 tablespoons (30g) of pesto into each portion of an ice cube tray. Cover and freeze overnight. Pop the pesto cubes out and place in a freezer-safe resealable bag. Store frozen for up to 3 months.

THAI-STYLE VINAIGRETTE

CJ'S STREET FOOD—MARK THOMAS—RALEIGH/DURHAM, NC

MAKES 4 ½ CUPS (1060ML)

Mark Thomas of CJ's Street Food considers this Thai-Style Vinaigrette to be his workhorse sauce. It's an integral component of his Asian-style slaw, a staple he uses on his fish and pork tacos, chicken burritos and several other menu items. "It adds a complex, light acidic flavor, which works really well with anything that is fatty or creamy," he says. "It helps balance all the flavors and textures on your palate, which is what I shoot for on every item."

---

1 cup (237ml) lime juice

1 shallot, minced

2 tsp (10g) minced ginger

2 tsp (7g) minced garlic

1 tsp (7g) vanilla extract or 1 vanilla bean, split, with the seeds scraped out

2 tsp (14g) honey

2 tsp (10g) kosher salt

2 tsp (10g) fish sauce

3 cups (710ml) vegetable or canola oil

In a blender, add the lime juice, shallot, ginger, garlic, vanilla, honey, salt and fish sauce. The blades should just be covered with liquid. Add more lime juice depending on the design of your blender.

Blend all the ingredients for at least 1 minute. The friction from the blender blades will create heat that will take the raw edge off the garlic and ginger as well as help the honey blend uniformly and release the oils from the vanilla seeds.

While the blender is running, slowly drizzle the oil into the center of the blender. It should look like a cyclone spinning. As the oil is drizzled into the cyclone, it will begin to tighten up and become smaller. Once all the oil is added, blend for another 20 seconds to make sure everything is incorporated.

Depending on the fish sauce, you may need to adjust to your taste. If it is too acidic, add more honey. If it is too salty, add a little more oil to thin it out. Add more lime if the flavor isn't strong enough. Use more fish sauce to season if you need more punch.

ROAD TRIP JOURNAL

BY TERRI PHILLIPS

This cookbook has been an exercise primarily in traversing distances. With Kim and Phil based in San Francisco, and myself in Portland, Oregon, we've become accustomed to collaborating with all the tools and tricks the current digital age offers. Skype, Google Docs, FaceTime: you name it, we've used it. But when it came time to take photographs of the chefs, owners and the dishes they prepare on food carts and trucks in 12 cities scattered throughout the United States, there was only one way to do it: a classic road trip. Months of meticulous planning and one successful Kickstarter campaign later, and we were on the road. In keeping with the tradition of our blog, we wanted to ensure that the food and sights captured in this book are authentically from the chefs and owners themselves.

Kim and Phil had photographed the California carts first, all that was left for us to do was drive the 2,226 miles from Austin to New York. Before the 17 days spent traversing the lower half of the United States the term "road trip" was heavy with expectations formed from all my favorite books and movies. Scenes of screaming lyrics to music with the windows down, playing ridiculous car games, eating terrible gas station jerky and corn nuts and stopping at every World's Giant Ball of Twine kept me wide-eyed and impatient every night for weeks leading up to our departure.

The cities themselves carried their own automatic promise: New Orleans, Washington D.C., New York City. Those, I knew, would contain enough sights and experiences to fill in a lifetime of awkward silences at parties (something I never seem to be short of), but it was the travel in between destinations I really itched for. The offbeat rural areas, the miles and miles of road, the sense of rootlessness, waking up in a new place every morning with a brief moment of being completely unsure which state you're looking at through the hotel window. This was what I felt would come to satiate my appetite for adventure.

The cities delivered and then some. New Orleans was a feast. I've never seen a city so tragically beautiful in every detail. We caught them as they were gearing up for Mardi Gras, and the sheer abandon of the nighttime festivities felt as relieving as a belly laugh. Washington D.C. was much more austere, the memorials and monuments impressive with their solemnity and the sheer weight of their history. New York City was constant adrenaline. There is no strolling or stopping to gape in New York, it's cramming in as many sights and sounds as you can while being carried along by the crowd. I could have spent months in every city we'd visited and I still would have felt like I'd only gotten a taste.

Each location flew by in a blur. Our tight schedule kept us always on the move, constantly navigating hotel rooms and unfamiliar streets. One 24-hour stretch had us leaving New Orleans in time to sink into grateful sleep in an Atlanta bed. The next morning would see us up early shooting a food truck, then driving three hours to Charlotte, North Carolina to meet another friendly, fascinating mobile chef, and then driving another three hours to Raleigh. Though Raleigh and Durham was one of our busiest stops with six food trucks in one day, they banded together to figure out one spot to *drive to us*. Words can't express the gratitude we felt toward this touchingly close-knit food truck community.

But I was surprised to find the feeling of roaming I had looked forward to so much, the sense of being ready for anything, of having each day brings its own setting change, didn't come from the days and days spent on the road. If anything, that just drove home how homogenized the United States freeways have become. Drop me on a stretch of freeway in North Carolina and I would have been hard-pressed to claim with any certainty I wasn't in Oregon. (At least until I noticed the Waffle Houses every couple of miles.) Instead I found that rootless sense of adventure in the tiny kitchens of the food trucks themselves.

These food trucks gave me exactly what was lacking in the all-too-beaten paths of the freeways: a glimpse behind the curtain of each city. More than the Creole flair Kami's Philly-inspired Korean cheesesteak, the attitude of each city toward its burgeoning food truck community was as revealing as its cuisine. We heard stories of turf wars and death threats, of criminal summonses over arbitrary impossible-to-avoid laws, of necessary back-alley purchases of black market permits. But we especially loved seeing the camaraderie between food trucks; often exchanging food with each other and supporting each other through the tough times (there are many). We see them banding together to form coalitions and putting together food truck-themed events.

Our journey from Austin to New York City gave us a crash course into a wide spectrum of American cities. While some cities choose to embrace this new mobile food movement, other cities choose to make it almost impossible to operate. But one thing is certain. The perception of "fine dining" and "food truck" is changing for the better. As these passionate folks fire up their kitchens and work to stamp out the term "roach coach" once and for all, they're finding clientele lining up outside their windows, eager to have their perceptions changed.

The cross-country flight back to Portland from New York was quiet as we each processed the whirlwind of the previous two-and-a-half weeks. Our suitcases were crammed with food truck T-shirts and our phones were pushing the limits of our data plans. We were exhausted and at least ten pounds heavier apiece. But our silence was underscored with a sense of accomplishment. We did it. We visited eleven more food carts in Portland and overall worked with 63 food carts for this book. It was a lot harder than we expected, but we loved every call, email, tweet, word, photo and moment that it took to complete this cookbook. We hope it brings you as much enjoyment as it has brought to us.

FOOD CARTS FEATURED IN THIS BOOK

CALIFORNIA

LOS ANGELES

The Chili Philosopher
Alex Kavallierou
chiliphilosopher.com

Flat Iron
Timothy Mark Abell
flatirontruck.com

Rosa's Bella Cucina
Rosa Graziano
rosasbellacucina.com

Tokyo Doggie Style
Chef Keith Yokoyama and
Allie Yamamoto
tokyodoggiestyle.com

The Urban Oven
Scott Tremonti
theurbanoven.com

SAN FRANCISCO BAY AREA

333 Truck
San Jose, CA
Eric Chung
333truck.com

Doc's of the Bay
Oakland, CA
Zak Silverman
docsofthebay.com

Eat Fuki
San Francisco, CA
Alex Meisels, Seabrook Gubbins
and Chef Craig Peterson
eatfuki.com

Fat Face
Davis, CA
Jaymes Luu
fatfacedavis.com

Garden Creamery
San Francisco, CA
Erin Lang and Donald Capozzi
gardencreamery.com

Hill Country Barbecue
Redwood City, CA
John Capelo
hillcountrybbq.net

JapaCurry
San Francisco, CA
Jay Hamada
japacurry.com

Melts My Heart
San Jose, CA
Owners: Brian Aflague and Linda Tran
Chef: Wes Isip
meltsmyhearttruck.com

Sam's ChowderMobile
Half Moon Bay, CA
Paul and Julie Shenkman and
Lewis Rossman
samschowdermobile.com

Waffle Amore
San Jose, CA
Judy Vandoorne
waffleamore.com

WhipOul!
Emeryville, CA
Owner: Rob John
Chef: Brett Downey
facebook.com/WhipOutFoodTruck

GEORGIA

ATLANTA

MIX'D UP Food Truck
Brett Eanes
mixdupfoods.com

LOUISIANA

NEW ORLEANS

Frencheeze Food Truck
Jason Robinson King and Myrialis King
and Bootz
frencheezefoodtruck.com

La Cocinita Food Truck
Benoit Angulo and Rachel Billow
lacocinitafoodtruck.com

Meltdown
Michelle Weaver
meltdownpops.com

NOLA Girl Food Truck and Catering
Dannielle Judie
nolagirlfood.com

Rue Chow
Jarett and Rachel Eymard
ruechow.com

NEW YORK

NEW YORK CITY

Big D's Grub Truck
Dennis Kum
facebook.com/bigdsgrub

The Cinnamon Snail
Adam Sobel
cinnamonsnail.com

La Bella Torte
Joe and Anne Marie Glaser
facebook.com/labellatorte

Lumpia Shack
Neil Syham and Angie Roca
lumpiashacknyc.com

Mayhem and Stout
Steve Applegate and Jay Brown
mayhemandstout.com

Parantha Alley
Rajeev Yerneni and Retu Singla
twitter.com/paranthaalley

Phil's Steaks
Jim Drew, J.J. Jensen, and Kevin and
Mla McConnell
philssteaks.com

The Treats Truck
Kim Ima
treatstruck.com

NORTH CAROLINA

CHARLOTTE

The Herban Legend Mobile Café
Brian Seeley
theherbanlegend.com

RALEIGH/DURHAM

American Meltdown
Paul and Alycia Inserra
americanmeltdown.org

Barone Meatball Company
Stephen Dewey
baronemeatball.com

Café Prost
Stephan and Nicole Bayer
cafeprost.com

CJ's Street Food
Mark Thomas
cjstreetfood.com

Deli-icious
Susan Tower
deliicioustruck.com

Pie Pushers
Mike and Becky Hacker
piepushers.com

Porchetta
Chefs Matthew Hayden and
Nicholas Crosson
porchettardu.com

MINNESOTA

MINNEAPOLIS

The Moral Omnivore
Ross & Linnea Logas
themoralomnivore.com

Gai Gai Thai
Kris Petcharawises
facebook.com/gaigaithai

OREGON

PORTLAND

Big-Ass Sandwiches
Brian and Lisa Wood
bigasssandwiches.com

Carte Blanche
Jessie Aron
carteblanchefoodcart.com

Caspian Kabob
Victor Darchini
kabobpdx.com

Chickpeadx
Yair Maidan
chickpeadx.com

The Egg Carton
Tim and Sarah Arkwright
facebook.com/eggcartonpdx

Fried Egg I'm in Love
Chef/Owner: Jace Krause
Owner: Ryan Lynch
friedegglove.com

Moberi
Ryan Carpenter
moberismoothies.com

Nong's Khao Man Gai
Nong Poonsukwattana
kmgpdx.com

Rua
Jason Myers
ruapdx.com

Savor Soup House
Adam Dunn and Colleen Schroht
savorsouphouse.com

Thrive: Sauce and Bowls
Erika Reagor
thrivepacificnw.com

PENNSYLVANIA

PHILADELPHIA

HubBub Coffee Company
Drew Crockett
hubbubcoffee.com

KAMI (Korean American
Menus Inspired)
Jin Jang
twitter.com/KAMI19104

Lil' Pop Shop
Jeanne Chang, Kate Gallagher
and Vince Tseng
lilpopshop.com

Poi Dog Philly
Kiki Aranita and Chris Vacca
poidogphilly.com

Taco Mondo
Michael Sultan and Carolyn Nguyen
twitter.com/tacomondo

The Tot Cart
Julie Crist
twitter.com/TheTotCart

TEXAS

AUSTIN

Fishey Bizness Seafood Co.
Owners: Dennis and Sylvia White
Chefs: Dennis, Justin, and
Brandon White
Fisheybiznessatx.com

Guac N Roll
Benjamin and Ashlea Miller
guacnrollaustin.com

Love Balls Bus
Sao and Gabe Rothschild
loveballsbus.com

The Peached Tortilla
Eric Silverstein
thepeachedtortilla.com

WASHINGTON, D.C.

El Fuego DC
Chef/Owner: Manuel Alfaro
Chefs: Omar Rodriguez Valladares
and Nestor Augusto Rodriguez
facebook.com/elfuegodc

Hula Girl Truck
Mikala Brennan
hulagirltruck.com

ACKNOWLEDGMENTS

We would like to thank all the hardworking chefs and owners who contributed their recipes and stories. This book is for you and it would not have happened without you letting people in on your lives and treasured recipes. A big heartfelt thank-you goes out to William Kiester, Marissa Giambelluca and Meg Baskis of Page Street Publishing for making the dream of writing and photographing our own book a reality. We're still shocked this is all happening. And thank you to our uber-talented friend Josh Iwata for our new logo and to our gorgeous friend Lavenda Memory for photographing us. We also could not be more honored to have Helen Rosner of *Saveur* magazine write our foreword.

Thanks to our friends who helped test our huge list of recipes: Michelle Chen, Majesta Patterson, Kristen Eberlin, Daisy Hsiung, Luci Chen, Misty White, Spencer Foxworth, Becca Iwata, Alisia Ray and Janis Smith. We're also super appreciative of Claudia and Derek Toomes for housing us in Raleigh, North Carolina, and Sarah Wesley and Donny Stevens for housing us in Portland, Oregon, when we were on our road trip to take pictures for this book. And much love goes to Bert Chen and Phil's sister, Michelle, for putting a roof over our heads as we pursue our dreams.

For the Kickstarter that helped fund our road trip, thanks to Zach Patterson for shooting the video and directing us to be as normal as possible. And we are so grateful to all the backers who helped fund our trip across the country, especially Diana Shen, Chris and Nancy Chen, Sally Phillips, Jennifer Ferrari and John Capelo, Maxyne Cho, Bert and Michelle Chen, Helen Yema Hosain, Donny, Martin Angulo, Lucille Chen, Evan Bowers and Kristen Eberlin, Olivia and Vi Ly, Joe and Maria Wood, Terry Armstrong, Zach and Majesta Patterson, Victor and Tracy Darchini, Sherritt Chowning, Jinal and Rikin Patel, LinhFu, Arthur and Maggie, James and Isabella Yang, Noriko and David Raffauf, Sharon Davis, Michael Payne, Julie Shieh, Amy and Greg Allen, the Vance/Connelly family, Teri Salway, Daisy Hsiung, and Claudia and Derek Toomes.

And finally, thanks to all our followers who helped push us to keep updating our blog.

ABOUT THE AUTHORS

Behind the Food Carts is a blog started by Kim Pham and Phil Shen in Portland, Oregon. Now based in the San Francisco Bay Area, Kim and Phil are professional photographers and videographers under their studio name KIM+PHIL Photography. The team is completed by Terri Phillips, a content writer based in Portland, Oregon. When not blogging, Kim and Phil enjoy movies with subtitles, Ping-Pong and hunting for vintage Polaroid cameras at flea markets. Terri enjoys curating her collection of microbrew bottles, running from zombies and building Lego sets with her son Zane. Behind the Food Carts has more than 200,000 followers on Tumblr and was named *Saveur* magazine's Best Culinary Travel Blog in 2013.

BehindtheFoodCarts.com